Defining and Developing Proficiency: Guidelines, Implementations, and Concepts

Edited by Heidi Byrnes and Michael Canale

In conjunction with the American Council on the Teaching of Foreign Languages

National Textbook Company, *Lincolnwood, Illinois U.S.A.*

Contents

Introduction

Heidi Byrnes
Georgetown University
Michael Canale
Ontario Institute for
Studies in Education

The most thorough critical reviews of ACTFL's initiatives to help define, assess, and develop language proficiency have reached a significant common conclusion: it is the call for systematic and rigorous research on the *ACTFL Proficiency Guidelines*, as well as on their potential impact on teaching methodology, curriculum design, and evaluation. Serious concerns about ACTFL's efforts have been eloquently and persuasively voiced by Savignon (1), Lantolf and Frawley (2), and Bachman and Savignon (3), for example. Perhaps such eloquence and persuasiveness have been paralleled in the writings of the growing number of proponents of the proficiency movement. Be that as it may, the danger with any movement is that a rhetoric of fear and enthusiasm will develop which is more likely to misrepresent and confuse than to clarify the crucial issues. As ACTFL's work generates even more discussion, it would be wise to change the character of the debate from rhetoric to research, that is, to efforts toward delineating testable hypotheses which could form the basis for substantive and replicable work on the numerous questions surrounding ACTFL/ETS proficiency testing, particularly as these relate to an instructed language acquisition context. The contents of this volume not only

Heidi Byrnes (Ph.D., Georgetown University) is Associate Professor of German at Georgetown University. She is a certified tester and master trainer for the ACTFL/ETS method of assessing oral proficiency in German. Her article "Second Language Acquisition: Insights from a Proficiency Orientation" is included in this volume.

Michael Canale (Ph.D., McGill University) has taught English as a second language and French as a second language through adult education services in Haiti and Montreal. At present, he is Associate Professor in the Curriculum Department and in the Center for Franco-Ontarian Studies at the Ontario Institute for Studies in Education (OISE) and the University of Toronto. Since joining OISE in 1976, he has directed research projects dealing with French language maintenance and education in a minority setting, development of French language enrichment materials, communicative competence, microcomputers in language learning, and assessment of language proficiency in minority and majority settings. His most recent publications are as coauthor of *The TOEFL from a Communicative Viewpoint on Language Proficiency: A Working Paper* and as author of *Microcomputer Software for Language Arts: Survey and Analysis*.

represent an important milestone in the proficiency movement but also provide ACTFL's and others' clearest response yet to the call for a more systematic and rigorous research program.

The volume begins with a very concrete example of ACTFL's leadership and achievement in the proficiency movement: the new generic *ACTFL Proficiency Guidelines*, appended to the first paper by David V. Hiple. This paper traces historical constellations which were operational in the development of the provisional guidelines of 1982. The intent is not so much to establish their chronological sequencing but to elucidate some factors inside, as well as outside, the profession that delimited, to some extent, which issues were addressed and how they were being addressed. In their own way, the 1986 *ACTFL Proficiency Guidelines*, too, reflect diverse concerns. Therefore, in calling for an active research component, Hiple clearly anticipates and invites refinements to this document as well.

The contribution by Vicki Galloway represents a thorough investigation of perhaps the key concerns in conjunction with the proficiency movement—namely, its possible extension to the notion of curriculum design, the elaboration of syllabuses, the formulation of appropriate classroom procedures, and ultimately, the preparation of pedagogical materials. She carefully examines a number of issues which are involved in moving from product assessments to process recommendations as the practice of foreign language teaching presupposes them. Her discussion clearly advises reflected action as the profession rapidly embarks on this critical phase of the proficiency movement.

While well-motivated applications of insights from proficiency testing in a classroom environment take center stage in the Galloway paper, Patricia Dandonoli reports on efforts to shore up the testing component itself. Her contribution provides insights into the issues that must be addressed by two significant shifts in proficiency testing: away from oral proficiency testing toward the testing of receptive skills, particularly reading; and away from the direct person-to-person testing that characterizes the oral interview toward a computerized adaptive testing, which not only allows wide application of the method of assessment but also provides a significant data source into numerous aspects which must be clarified as a theory of language proficiency is being developed.

One specific instance of the need for clarification is addressed in the paper by James R. Child. In proposing an independent typology of texts, he focuses on one problem area that the current descriptions of proficiency in all four language modes can easily encounter: the potential circularity of argument as functional use is being defined in terms of text types and, in turn, text types by the kinds of operations learners are likely to be able to perform when confronted with them.

The volume concludes with an urgent call for proficiency-related research by Heidi Byrnes. The intent is to attract SLA researchers to the multiplicity of issues surrounding proficiency as it has been delineated under the ACTFL/ETS system of assessment. Among these are its use as a summative statement about functional language ability, its contributing factors and their relative weight at different stages of language learning, and its potential as a data resource which might help to shed light on such perennial problems as ultimate attainment, rate of acquisition, and fossilization. Ultimately, of course, such research aims to enable language professionals to provide the optimal learning environment for learners, in the area of methodology, syllabus and curriculum design, materials development, and standards of professional preparation and development.

The Need for Research

Each of the chapters in this volume underscores in its own way the importance of establishing specific research programs to monitor the new guidelines and their various implementations. To provide a more general design for initiating and coordinating systematic research on proficiency issues, ACTFL has outlined three main aspects of its own research program.* First, the major issues to be addressed are to include reliability and validity studies on the Oral Interview and other proficiency assessment instruments, studies on the effectiveness of current training procedures for use of these instruments, studies on the use of the guidelines in teaching methodology and curriculum design, and exploration of alternative ways of eliciting and measuring language proficiency. Second, implementation of the research program will include both in-house projects, a visiting scholar program at ACTFL, and contracts with outside research agencies. Finally, a sustained effort will be made to focus the profession's attention on the nature and importance of high-quality research in second language education. To this end, ACTFL will create a special-interest group on research to meet at the annual ACTFL convention, a regularly published newsletter for those interested in the work of this group, periodic task forces on various research issues, and an annual listing in the *Foreign Language Annals* of abstracts of dissertation research relevant to language proficiency.

Of course, the research activities envisioned by ACTFL do not and should not exhaust the variety of relevant research studies required to monitor the proficiency movement. As an increasingly broad range of teachers, institutions, and students in different contexts look to proficiency as a potentially unifying concept, it will be necessary for other researchers and agencies to contribute to the research base. The following are some of the more important goals that have already surfaced as the proficiency movement gains prominence:
1. Comparative studies of similar movements outside the United States (for example, those in Australia, Canada, Great Britain, and Europe).
2. Studies of the relevance of the guidelines and their implementations in

language minority contexts (for example, within bilingual education programs in the United States and Europe, which typically serve children in the elementary grades).
3. The relevance of the current proficiency definitions, implementations, and concepts for self-directed and artistic uses of a second language (for example, language as a tool for thought or aesthetic exploration) rather than just for other-directed uses such as conversations and interviews.
4. Analysis of alternative approaches to the product-oriented, teacher-controlled, and highly structured formal assessment instruments currently associated with the proficiency movement (for example, alternatives such as incorporating oral interview tasks into unintrusive assessment and learning activities, into informal longitudinal monitoring and consultative approaches to assessment, or into self-assessment and learner-generated assessment activities).
5. Finally, analysis of the problems and strategies that emerge as learners engage in proficiency-oriented activities (for example, comparative analysis of problems and strategies at the cognitive, interactional, affective, and linguistic levels during an oral interview as opposed to those observed during learner interaction in group work).

Notes

*We are grateful to C. Edward Scebold, Executive Director of ACTFL, for providing this information.

References, Introduction

1. Savignon, Sandra J. "Evaluation of Communicative Competence: The ACTFL Provisional Proficiency Guidelines." *Modern Language Journal* 69, 2 (1985): 129–34.
2. Lantolf, James P., and William Frawley. "Oral-Proficiency Testing: A Critical Analysis." *Modern Language Journal* 69, 4 (1985):337–45.
3. Bachman, Lyle F., and Sandra J. Savignon. "The Evaluation of Communicative Language Proficiency: A Critique of the ACTFL Oral Interview and Suggestions for Its Revision and Development." Paper presented at the Perspectives on Proficiency Forum during the MLA convention, 29 December 1985, Chicago, IL.

1

A Progress Report on the ACTFL Proficiency Guidelines, 1982–1986

David V. Hiple
American Council on the
Teaching of Foreign Languages

Introduction

The creation of the President's Commission on Foreign Language and International Studies provided an unprecedented opportunity for diverse public and private groups to work together on setting future directions for the foreign language profession. The 1979 publication of *Strength through Wisdom*, the report of the President's commission, articulated the commission's findings "with a sense of great urgency" (13, p. 4), thus providing publicity for the profession and presenting a set of recommendations on which to act.

In issuing its charge, the commission lamented the existence of complacency and defeatism in the profession and cited an interrelated downward spiral of reduced funding, declining enrollments, and further reduced funding. The commission expressed the hope that this decline in foreign language enrollments might be supplanted by the advent of "true yardsticks of national requirements in determining enrollments, employment policies, and the capabilities of research facilities" (13, p. 5). Woodford (14, p. 73), in a background paper for the commission, had recommended "the adoption and acceptance of a common yardstick, a series of descriptors of foreign language ability that are based on real life performance."

David V. Hiple (A.B.D. Rutgers University) is a Project Director for ACTFL. He has participated in the development of the ACTFL Proficiency Guidelines and has organized and conducted numerous oral proficiency testing workshops. Past experience includes language teaching and test development at Educational Testing Service.

Most of the commission's foreign language recommendations are linked to this fundamental premise.

This chapter chronicles ACTFL's response to the recommendations of the President's commission through the creation of the Provisional Proficiency Guidelines (1). In reviewing those recommendations, the vagueness of the commissions's charge and the resulting problems in the provisional guidelines will be examined. This chapter also presents revised generic proficiency guidelines and discusses their evolution as a result of experimentation and recommendations from the foreign language teaching profession.

Background

The concept of nationally recognized performance or proficiency standards, as advocated by the President's commission, was not without precedent. In 1977 the Modern Language Association (MLA) and the American Council of Learned Societies (ACLS) obtained support from both the Rockefeller Foundation and the National Endowment for the Humanities to form five task forces: (1) the Task Force on Institutional Language Policy, (2) the Task Force on the Commonly Taught Languages, (3) the Task Force on the Less Commonly Taught Languages, (4) the Task Force on Public Awareness, and (5) the Task Force on Government Relations. The task forces worked in these separate but related areas with the goal of proposing to the profession "a unifying principle, a sense of mission, and a set of educational objectives on which to focus its energies" (Brod, 3, p. 4).

In fact, preparation of the Task Forces' recommendations, *Language Study for the 1980s: Reports of the MLA-ACLS Language Task Forces,* coincided with preparations for the appointment of the President's Commission on Foreign Language and International Studies. As Brod (3, p. 4) indicates, "most of [the task forces'] recommendations were ready for the President's Commission when it held its first meeting in October 1978." Thus, the recommendations of the MLA-ACLS task forces influenced those of the President's commission, which in turn influenced the rationale of the ACTFL proficiency guidelines proposal, *A Design for Measuring and Communicating Foreign Language Proficiency (2),* funded in 1981 by the U.S. Department of Education.

Reviewing the seminal recommendations of both the MLA-ACLS task forces and the President's commission, the reader is struck by the casual and sometimes almost contradictory use of such terms as *performance standards, proficiency standards,* and *achievement goals.* Of the nineteen final recommendations of the MLA-ACLS task forces, drawn from the individual task force reports, recommendations 1 and 8 (Brod, 3, p. 5) most specifically addressed the setting of standards as follows:

- Institutions and, where appropriate, state educational systems should be encouraged to adopt nationally recognized performance or proficiency standards.

- A set of standards should be developed by the various professional language groups, in association with testing organizations, whereby achieved proficiency at the various stages of language acquisition can be determined in ways that are universally accepted and understood.

Of the final recommendations of the President's commission, those relating to the establishment of a National Criteria and Assessment Program (13, p. 13) most specifically addressed the setting of standards:

- Assess the proficiency of both students and teachers in existing as well as new or experimental foreign language programs.
- Determine the language skills required to function in a variety of contexts.
- Establish language proficiency achievement goals for the end of each year of study at all levels, with special attention to speaking proficiency.

Thus, the great impetus in the profession during 1980–1981 to respond to the charge of the President's commission lacked a clear direction. Was a year-by-year and/or level-by-level achievement-oriented document desired? Or, since the term *proficiency* was invoked, was an extraclassroom, functionally oriented document being advocated?

Given the cloudiness of and the apparent conflict in the commission's charge, the profession could be expected to interpret the recommendations in various ways. The charge that had emerged seemed to serve two masters. On the one hand, it called for a document that would enable the profession to assess performance based on actual proficiency, "rather than by the number of hours spent in the classroom" (13, p. 13). On the other hand, this document was intended to enable the profession to set achievement goals "for the end of each year of study at all levels." Could a document, a common yardstick, be designed that would articulate a progressive or graduated sequence of functional language learning stages, and could the charge be met in such a way that would give special attention to speaking proficiency?

The Development of the ACTFL Provisional Proficiency Guidelines

In addition to the lack of clarity surrounding the charge, there were other obstacles hampering a meaningful response to the recommendations of the President's commission. One was the availability of resources. In making its recommendations, the President's commission had targeted a funding source and envisioned a competition among institutional applicants for a contract to administer a National Criteria and Assessment Program, but neither the program nor the funding materialized.

Clifford (5) proposed that a consortium of professional organizations launch an academic language proficiency program. Indeed, shortly after the conclusion of the Foreign Service Institute (FSI) Testing Kit Workshops (see Frith, 7), a meeting was called to discuss the creation of such a consortium to continue language proficiency activities in the academic community. Of the organizations represented at this meeting, ACTFL elected to pursue the initiation of language proficiency projects, and in early 1981 two interrelated grant proposals were funded by the U.S. Department of Education. One project, to offer academic oral proficiency tester training, was designed to respond to the commission's charge of assessing the proficiency of both students and teachers and was undertaken in collaboration with Educational Testing Service (ETS). The other project was designed to respond to the commission's charge of creating "language proficiency achievement goals" and was undertaken in collaboration with the Modern Language Association.

Another constraint was the grant proposal procedure itself. A proposal cannot be equivocal, nor can it express doubt about the task that is to be undertaken. It must exhibit a certain degree of salesmanship. In addition to making a case conceptually, a proposal must also make a case concretely, dealing with timelines, budgets, and deliverables. Since the submitted document must also compete with others for what are often very limited funds, a proposal must convince the readers and, ultimately, the funders that they will receive the greatest return on their investment by funding the proposal in question, as opposed to another in the competition.

The funded proposal to "create generic proficiency goals for reading, writing, speaking, listening, and culture" and "language-specific sets of proficiency goals—in French, German, and Spanish—all of which would be based on the generic goals . . . " (2, p. 14) called for the delivery of these goals in one year. Working committees were to be formed first to create generic statements by skill area and subsequently to make language-specific applications. ACTFL posited in the proposal that it would not be propitious to construct proficiency goals for the "commonly taught" and the "less commonly taught" languages simultaneously, but that work should be undertaken in a fashion which would draw initially upon the knowledge base in the commonly taught languages and then extended to those less commonly taught. ACTFL also suggested that once these newly constructed goals became available, other professional problems, such as the articulation of curricula, the design of learning activities, and the identification of instructional methods, could be addressed. This second supposition was meant to respond to the duality of the commission's recommendations, which seemed to be calling for an all-purpose document to be utilized for evaluative objectives, as well as curricular objectives.

In arguing for the funding of the proposal, ACTFL made the following reference (2, p. 6) to the commission's report, linking the project design to the commission's recommendations:

> This proposal outlines a series of well-defined activities which will continue to broaden the significance of the work of the President's Commission and respond to the specific recommendation that foreign language educators need to better define the goals and objectives of language programs by establishing specific proficiency goals for their instruction and developing appropriate measuring devices to communicate to students their attainment of these objectives.

As the project came to life, a number of factors influenced the form of the "language proficiency goals" that had been promised. It will be remembered that the initial ACTFL project to train academic oral proficiency testers was being conducted simultaneously, and from the outset, interest in tester training was intense and widespread. This interest served to make the production of assessment-focused statements, particularly those referring to oral proficiency assessment, a priority. The greatest reservoir of experience in creating such assessment-focused statements resided in the government, and it was only natural that the project would draw on that expertise. The emphasis in government had been on oral assessment, largely because of the living tradition of the oral interview. Since "special attention to speaking proficiency" had been strongly recommended by the President's commission as well, such an emphasis did not seem in violation of the charge.

Another factor that influenced the oral proficiency assessment focus of the ACTFL language proficiency goals was the outcome of a grant-funded research project, known as the Common Yardstick Project, conducted at Educational Testing Service to investigate the feasibility of establishing national academic standards for oral proficiency. After careful investigation, ETS endorsed the government oral proficiency scale but made two changes to adapt that scale for academic use. The first adaptation concerned combining the upper levels of the government scale into one broad category, since few academic language learners reach the upper ranges of oral proficiency during formal study (see Carroll, 4); the second recommendation concerned further subdividing the lower ranges of oral proficiency, since most academic language learners cluster there, and the government scale cannot discriminate finely enough among them (see Liskin-Gasparro, 9). The Common Yardstick Project produced initial oral proficiency descriptions for these newly created levels, and the expanded oral proficiency scale and the accompanying level descriptions served as a conceptual model for the new ACTFL project.

For a number of reasons (in response to the explicit recommendation of the President's commission, as an outgrowth of the FSI Testing Kit Workshops, due to the influence of the Common Yardstick Project, or perhaps because of the intrinsic appeal of the oral interview), the 1982 provisional guidelines reflected an emphasis on oral proficiency. Comparable attention to receptive skills proficiency seems to have lagged behind, in part at least, because of the lack of assessment instruments to permit evaluation of performance against criteria. Eisner (6, p. 5) refers to the fact that what is tested is what is considered important or conversely, " . . . the fields not tested are considered less important than those that are . . . ."

Thus, an assessment-focused document evolved that, while addressing the four skills and culture, also served as a support document for tester training and oral proficiency evaluation. The achievement-focused side of the charge, the "goals for the end of each year of study at all levels," gradually became a secondary (if not impossible) objective of the project. In this vein, the document came to be referred to as "guidelines," since "goals" was no longer an accurate description. In retrospect, then, one might say that, as ACTFL elected to defer to the President's commission by accepting its dual concerns, an assessment-focused document became compromised by an impossible charge, namely to create "language proficiency achievement goals for the end of each year of study at all levels."

Strengths and Weaknesses

The *ACTFL Provisional Proficiency Guidelines* was first circulated publicly at the 1982 ACTFL Annual Meeting in New York with subsequent distribution to ACTFL and ADFL (Association of Departments of Foreign Languages) memberships and through the ACTFL Materials Center and professional publications. The guidelines have generated a great deal of interest not only in proficiency testing but also in proficiency-based curriculum development and instruction.

Hummel (8, pp. 13–14) holds that the notion underlying the guidelines is revolutionary, and he identifies three innovative aspects: (1) "students can be evaluated, not by the number of courses passed, but by the level of actual proficiency attained"; (2) "separate ratings for proficiency in various skills provide profiles of discrete abilities rather than a single, global evaluation"; and (3) " . . . the generic guidelines describe somewhat impressionistically criteria that yield a picture of gradually increasing skill in communication . . . ." At the same time, however, he has expressed a concern that the curricular objective of the guidelines obtrudes on the evaluative objective: "You can't have it both ways. . . . To the degree that guidelines depend on instructional presuppositions, their value as a standard of measurement is vitiated."

The curricular objective, the "achievement goals" that the President's commission called for, cannot coexist with the evaluative objective, the assessment of proficiency. Yet, while proficiency guidelines cannot serve as curriculum guidelines, proficiency guidelines can provide curricular direction by imparting a progressive sequence of realistic expectations (see Galloway, this volume).

Valuable input from the field identified a variety of changes and refinements to be made in the provisional guidelines. Hummel commented on the undue intrusion of the productive domain on the receptive domain and the tendency to tie general cognitive skills, such as inferencing, to hierarchical proficiency levels. In regard to the culture guidelines, a range of revisions was proposed from the field.

Fundamental issues had presented themselves as the project committees set to the task initially. There was the challenge of trying to construct a hierarchy of culture skills. Did culture skills even build progressively? There was the nagging issue of "small c" versus "large C" culture. Where did the two become integrated? Moreover, there was the question of whether culture proficiency could be quantified in the same fashion as the other proficiencies and defined by ranges of ability—while the other areas are essentially skill-based, the culture component is essentially content-based.

Lowe (10, p. 32) reminded readers: "The ILR scale has existed for only thirty years. The ACTFL/ETS scale has existed for three." The ILR work served as a very useful referent for the working committees as they created proficiency statements in the four skill areas. In the case of culture, however, no ILR-endorsed model existed, and the ideal model for the quantification of culture proficiency remained elusive. Until clearer notions emerge regarding what constitutes culture proficiency, it seems premature to advance the existing model any further. ACTFL is currently seeking funding to address this issue in more depth in a separate project.

In 1983, ACTFL received support from the Department of Education to initiate the second stage of the guidelines project to create language-specific sets of proficiency statements for Chinese, Japanese, and Russian, using the generic guidelines as a model. As the working committees began the task, however, an Indo-European bias in the generic guidelines became more and more problematic. Each level description of the guidelines respects the functional trisection and contains function statements, context statements, and accuracy statements. The Western bias was most evident in statements that addressed the accuracy component of the trisection, but different issues emerged from skill area to skill area. A revision of the Provisional Proficiency Guidelines was not among the objectives of the funded project, but after completing the initial draft of the Chinese, Japanese, and Russian statements, it became evident that creating meaningful guidelines for those languages might not be possible without a revision of the generic guidelines. Thus, ACTFL petitioned the Department of Education and was granted an amendment to the project to revise the generic guidelines and to create, in turn, viable guidelines for Chinese, Japanese, and Russian. As an additional benefit, the revision of the generic guidelines enabled ACTFL to undertake the revision of the French, German, and Spanish guidelines, as well.

Generous support from the Department of Education made it possible for ACTFL to undertake a systematic revision of the provisional guidelines. Careful scrutiny by the profession had clarified their strengths and weaknesses and brought about changes and refinements, such as the separation of achievement-focused statements from an assessment-focused document, the neutralizing of the undue influence of the productive skill descriptions on the receptive skill descriptions, and the correction of the Indo-European bias.

Proficiency Guidelines, 1986

Woodford (14, 73), in a background paper for the President's commission, identified the following professional areas that he considered important:

> Needs fall into three major areas: (1) the adoption and acceptance of a common yardstick, a series of descriptors of foreign language ability that are based on real life performance; (2) training programs and materials to prepare teachers to evaluate pupil progress within their own foreign language programs; (3) development of receptive skills tests, listening and reading, that can be administered nationally requiring no special skill in test administration or extraordinary expense.

Having previously addressed the first two areas identified by Woodford, ACTFL began to focus on the third, namely to develop receptive skills tests. ACTFL has initiated a project to develop a battery of computer-adaptive reading and listening proficiency tests (see Dandonoli, this volume). Just as the oral proficiency test prompted an emphasis on the oral descriptions in the 1982 provisional guidelines, the forthcoming reading and listening proficiency tests reflect a shift toward those skill areas in the 1986 guidelines. Thus, the 1986 guidelines are intended to be more balanced in their coverage of the various language skill areas.

A number of concepts were considered with the goal of making the receptive skill area descriptions independent of the productive skill area descriptions. An effort was made to uncouple the relationship between text length and level of proficiency. In the speaking definitions, for example, length of utterance is an important factor in defining level of proficiency, but in the case of the receptive skills, length cannot play the same role, since a lengthier selection with more extralinguistic support may, in fact, be less difficult than a shorter selection with less extralinguistic support. Furthermore, an effort was made not only to acknowledge the importance of the context in which a text may be presented but also the degree of knowledge and interest an individual may bring to a text, either written or aural, since context, interest, and extratextual knowledge can have a great effect on what is understood (see Smith, 11).

The 1986 Proficiency Guidelines seek to take into account an individual's interaction with a text "on level" as well as with a text "at a slightly higher level where context and/or extralinguistic background knowledge are supportive" (Novice-High, reading). In the case of listening, the 1986 guidelines reflect an attempt to discriminate more clearly between interactive contexts and noninteractive contexts, "such as simple announcements and reports over the media" (Intermediate-Mid). The 1986 guidelines strive to respect the uniqueness of each skill area.

The most noticeable innovation of the 1986 Proficiency Guidelines may be further discrimination within the Superior range in the receptive skills: "Distinguished" has been added to describe Level 4 performance in the Superior range. Stevick (12) and Lowe (10) have commented on the likelihood that proficiency in the receptive skills will exceed proficiency in the active skills. Lowe (10, p. 35) indicated that, in the skill area of listening, the "offset" or the "comprehension advantage" represents the tendency in some languages for nonnatives to "understand more than they are able to say." In the case of reading, the justification for discrimination within the Superior level is particularly compelling. The traditional focus of upper division college foreign language instruction in the United States has been on preparing students to read and analyze literature, yet the provisional guidelines did not allow for the acknowledgment of "distinguished" reading proficiency.

Conclusion

The overriding characteristic of the 1986 ACTFL Proficiency Guidelines is that they are more truly generic because they delete or qualify language-specific references. This revision sets the stage for the six sets of language-specific guidelines that are forthcoming. The French, German, and Spanish guidelines will appear in a revised form, with Chinese, Japanese, and Russian guidelines being developed for the first time.

Finally, the word *provisional* does not appear on the revised guidelines. This is not to say that the 1986 guidelines are the definitive guidelines but rather to acknowledge that the construction and utilization of language proficiency guidelines is a dynamic, interactive process and that the academic sector, like the government sector, will periodically want to refine and update the criteria to reflect the needs of the users and the advances of the profession. The establishment of language proficiency guidelines is an ongoing research question and, in that sense, guidelines have important implications for research and, in turn, depend upon such research for continual refinement.

References, A Progress Report on the ACTFL Proficiency Guidelines, 1982–1986

1. *ACTFL Provisional Proficiency Guidelines.* Hastings-on-Hudson, NY: American Council on the Teaching of Foreign Languages, 1982.
2. *A Design for Measuring and Communicating Foreign Language Proficiency.* New York: American Council on the Teaching of Foreign Languages, 1981.
3. Brod, Richard I., ed. *Language Study for the 1980's: Reports of the MLA-ACLS Language Task Forces.* New York: The Modern Language Association, 1980.
4. Carroll, John B., et al. *The Foreign Language Attainments of Language Majors in the Senior Year: A Survey Conducted in U.S. Colleges and Universities.* Cambridge, MA: Graduate School of Education, Harvard University, 1967.
5. Clifford, Ray T. "Curricular and Comprehensive Program Evaluation," pp. 40–42 in Dale L. Lange, ed., *Proceedings of the National Conference on Professional Priorities.* New York: American Council on the Teaching of Foreign Languages, 1981.
6. Eisner, Elliot W. *The Educational Imagination on the Design and Evaluation of School Programs.* New York: Macmillan Publishing Co., 1979.
7. Frith, James R. "Testing the FSI Testing Kit." *ADFL Bulletin* 11 (1979):12–14.
8. Hummel, Robert D. "Evaluating Proficiency in Comprehension Skills: How Can We Measure What We Can't Observe?" *ADFL Bulletin* 16 (January 1985):13–16.
9. Liskin-Gasparro, Judith E. "The ACTFL Proficiency Guidelines: A Historical Perspective," pp. 11–42 in Theodore V. Higgs, ed., *Teaching for Proficiency, the Organizing Principle.* The ACTFL Foreign Language Education Series. Lincolnwood, IL: National Textbook Co., 1984.
10. Lowe, Pardee, Jr. "The ILR Scale as a Synthesizing Research Principle: The View from the Mountain," pp. 9–53 in Charles J. James, ed., *Foreign Language Proficiency in the Classroom and Beyond.* The ACTFL Foreign Language Education Series. Lincolnwood, IL: National Textbook Co., 1985.
11. Smith, Frank. *Psycholinguistics and Reading.* New York: Holt, Rinehart and Winston, 1978.
12. Stevick, Earl W. "Curriculum Development at the Foreign Service Institute," pp. 85–112 in Theodore V. Higgs, ed., *Teaching for Proficiency, the Organizing Principle.* The ACTFL Foreign Language Education Series. Lincolnwood, IL: National Textbook Co., 1984.
13. *Strength through Wisdom: A Critique of U.S. Capability. A Report to the President from the President's Commission on Foreign Language and International Studies.* Washington, D.C.: U.S. Government Printing Office, 1979.
14. Woodford, Protase. "Foreign Language Testing Background," pp. 71–77 in *President's Commission on Foreign Language and International Studies: Background Papers and Studies.* Washington, D.C.: U.S. Government Printing Office, 1979.

ACTFL Proficiency Guidelines 1986

The 1986 proficiency guidelines represent a hierarchy of global characterizations of integrated performance in speaking, listening, reading, and writing. Each description is a representative, not an exhaustive, sample of a particular range of ability, and each level subsumes all previous levels, moving from simple to complex in an "all-before-and-more" fashion.

Because these guidelines identify stages of proficiency, as opposed to achievement, they are not intended to measure what an individual has achieved through specific classroom instruction but rather to allow assessment of what an individual can and cannot do, regardless of where, when, or how the language has been learned or acquired; thus, the words *learned* and *acquired* are used in the broadest sense. These guidelines are not based on a particular linguistic theory or pedagogical method, since the guidelines are proficiency-based, as opposed to achievement-based, and are intended to be used for global assessment.

The 1986 guidelines should not be considered the definitive version, since the construction and utilization of language proficiency guidelines is a dynamic, interactive process. The academic sector, like the government sector, will continue to refine and update the criteria periodically to reflect the needs of the users and the advances of the profession. In this vein, ACTFL owes a continuing debt to the creators of the 1982 provisional proficiency guidelines and, of course, to the members of the Interagency Language Roundtable Testing Committee, the creators of the government's Language Skill Level Descriptions.

ACTFL would like to thank the following individuals for their contributions on this current guidelines project:

Heidi Byrnes
James Child
Nina Levinson
Pardee Lowe, Jr.
Seiichi Makino
Irene Thompson
A. Ronald Walton

These proficiency guidelines are the product of grants from the U.S. Department of Education.

Generic Descriptions–Speaking

Novice   The Novice level is characterized by an ability to communicate minimally with learned material.

Novice-Low   Oral production consists of isolated words and perhaps a few high-frequency phrases. Essentially no functional communicative ability.

15

Novice-Mid
Oral production continues to consist of isolated words and learned phrases within very predictable areas of need, although quantity is increased. Vocabulary is sufficient only for handling simple, elementary needs and expressing basic courtesies. Utterances rarely consist of more than two or three words and show frequent long pauses and repetition of interlocutor's words. Speaker may have some difficulty producing even the simplest utterances. Some Novice-Mid speakers will be understood only with great difficulty.

Novice-High
Able to satisfy partially the requirements of basic communicative exchanges by relying heavily on learned utterances but occasionally expanding these through simple recombinations of their elements. Can ask questions or make statements involving learned material. Shows signs of spontaneity, although this falls short of real autonomy of expression. Speech continues to consist of learned utterances rather than of personalized, situationally adapted ones. Vocabulary centers on areas such as basic objects, places, and most common kinship terms. Pronunciation may still be strongly influenced by first language. Errors are frequent and, in spite of repetition, some Novice-High speakers will have difficulty being understood even by sympathetic interlocutors.

Intermediate
The intermediate level is characterized by an ability to
—create with the language by combining and recombining learned elements, though primarily in a reactive mode;
—initiate, minimally sustain, and close in a simple way basic communicative tasks; and
—ask and answer questions.

Intermediate-Low
Able to handle successfully a limited number of interactive, task-oriented and social situations. Can ask and answer questions, initiate and respond to simple statements, and maintain face-to-face conversation, although in a highly restricted manner and with much linguistic inaccuracy. Within these limitations, can perform such tasks as introducing self, ordering a meal, asking directions, and making purchases. Vocabulary is adequate to express only the most elementary needs. Strong interference from native language may occur. Misunderstandings frequently arise, but with repetition, the Intermediate-Low speaker can generally be understood by sympathetic interlocutors.

Intermediate-Mid
Able to handle successfully a variety of uncomplicated, basic and communicative tasks and social situations. Can talk simply about self and family members. Can ask and answer questions and participate in simple conversations on topics beyond the most immediate needs; e.g., personal history and leisure-time activities. Utterance length increases slightly, but speech may continue to be characterized by frequent long pauses, since the smooth incorporation of even basic conversational strategies is often hindered as the speaker struggles to create appropriate language forms. Pronunciation may continue to be strongly influenced by first language and fluency may still be strained. Although misunderstandings still arise, the Intermediate-Mid speaker can generally be understood by sympathetic interlocutors.

Intermediate-High
Able to handle successfully most uncomplicated communicative tasks and social situations. Can initiate, sustain, and close a general conver-

sation with a number of strategies appropriate to a range of circumstances and topics, but errors are evident. Limited vocabulary still necessitates hesitation and may bring about slightly unexpected circumlocution. There is emerging evidence of connected discourse, particularly for simple narration and/or description. The Intermediate-High speaker can generally be understood even by interlocutors not accustomed to dealing with speaking at this level, but repetition may still be required.

Advanced

The Advanced level is characterized by an ability to
—converse in a clearly participatory fashion;
—initiate, sustain, and bring to closure a wide variety of communicative tasks, including those that require an increased ability to convey meaning with diverse language strategies due to a complication or an unforeseen turn of events;
—satisfy the requirements of school and work situations; and
—narrate and describe with paragraph-length connected discourse.

Advanced

Able to satisfy the requirements of everyday situations and routine school and work requirements. Can handle with confidence but not with facility complicated tasks and social situations, such as elaborating, complaining, and apologizing. Can narrate and describe with some details, linking sentences together smoothly. Can communicate facts and talk casually about topics of current public and personal interest, using general vocabulary. Shortcomings can often be smoothed over by communicative strategies, such as pause fillers, stalling devices, and different rates of speech. Circumlocution which arises from vocabulary or syntactic limitations very often is quite successful, though some groping for words may still be evident. The Advanced-level speaker can be understood without difficulty by native interlocutors.

Advanced-Plus

Able to satisfy the requirements of a broad variety of everyday, school, and work situations. Can discuss concrete topics relating to particular interests and special fields of competence. There is emerging evidence of ability to support opinions, explain in detail, and hypothesize. The Advanced-Plus speaker often shows a well-developed ability to compensate for an imperfect grasp of some forms with confident use of communicative strategies, such as paraphrasing and circumlocution. Differentiated vocabulary and intonation are effectively used to communicate fine shades of meaning. The Advanced-Plus speaker often shows remarkable fluency and ease of speech, but under the demands of Superior-level, complex tasks, language may break down or prove inadequate.

Superior

The Superior level is characterized by an ability to
—participate effectively in most formal and informal conversations on practical, social, professional, and abstract topics; and
—support opinions and hypothesize using native-like discourse strategies.

Superior

Able to speak the language with sufficient accuracy to participate effectively in most formal and informal conversations on practical, social, professional, and abstract topics. Can discuss special fields of competence and interest with ease. Can support opinions and hypothesize, but may not be able to tailor language to audience or discuss in depth highly abstract or unfamiliar topics. Usually the Superior-level speaker is only partially familiar with regional or other dialectical variants. The Superior-level speaker commands a wide variety of interactive strategies and shows good awareness of discourse strategies. The latter involves the ability to distinguish main ideas from supporting information through syntactic, lexical, and suprasegmental features (pitch, stress, intonation). Sporadic errors may occur, particularly in low-frequency structures and some complex high-frequency structures more common to formal writing, but no patterns of error are evident. Errors do not disturb the native speaker or interfere with communication.

Generic Descriptions–Listening

These guidelines assume that all listening tasks take place in an authentic environment at a normal rate of speech using standard or near-standard norms.

Novice The Novice level is characterized by an ability to recognize learned material and isolated words and phrases when strongly supported by context.

Novice-Low Understanding is limited to occasional isolated words, such as cognates, borrowed words, and high-frequency social conventions. Essentially no ability to comprehend even short utterances.

Novice-Mid Able to understand some short, learned utterances, particularly where context strongly supports understanding and speech is clearly audible. Comprehends some words and phrases from simple questions, statements, high-frequency commands, and courtesy formulae about topics that refer to basic personal information or the immediate physical setting. The listener requires long pauses for assimilation and periodically requests repetition and/or a slower rate of speech.

Novice-High Able to understand short, learned utterances and some sentence-length utterances, particularly where context strongly supports understanding and speech is clearly audible. Comprehends words and phrases from simple questions, statements, high-frequency commands, and courtesy formulae. May require repetition, rephrasing and/or a slowed rate of speech for comprehension.

Intermediate The Intermediate level is characterized by an ability to understand main ideas and some facts from interactive exchanges and simple connected aural texts.

Intermediate-Low Able to understand sentence-length utterances which consist of recombinations of learned elements in a limited number of content areas, particularly if strongly supported by the situational context. Content refers to basic personal background and needs, social conventions, and routine tasks, such as getting meals and receiving simple instructions and directions. Listening tasks pertain primarily to spontaneous face-to-face conversations. Understanding is often uneven; repetition and rewording may be necessary. Misunderstandings in both main ideas and details arise frequently.

Intermediate-Mid Able to understand sentence-length utterances which consist of recombinations of learned utterances on a variety of topics. Content continues to refer primarily to basic personal background and needs, social conventions, and somewhat more complex tasks, such as lodging, transportation, and shopping. Additional content areas include some personal interests and activities, and a greater diversity of instructions and directions. Listening tasks not only pertain to spontaneous face-to-face conversations but also to short routine telephone conversations and some deliberate speech, such as simple announcements and reports over the media. Understanding continues to be uneven.

Intermediate-High   Able to sustain understanding over longer stretches of connected discourse on a number of topics pertaining to different times and places; however, understanding is inconsistent due to failure to grasp main ideas and/or details. Thus, while topics do not differ significantly from those of an Advanced-level listener, comprehension is less in quantity and poorer in quality.

Advanced   The Advanced level is characterized by an ability to understand main ideas and most details of connected discourse on a variety of topics beyond the immediacy of the situation, including some topics where comprehension is complicated due to an unexpected sequence of events.

Advanced   Able to understand main ideas and most details of connected discourse on a variety of topics beyond the immediacy of the situation. Comprehension may be uneven due to a variety of linguistic and extralinguistic factors, among which topic familiarity is very prominent. These texts frequently involve description and narration in different time frames or aspects, such as present, nonpast, habitual, or imperfective. Texts may include interviews, short lectures on familiar topics, and news items and reports primarily dealing with factual information. Listener is aware of cohesive devices but may not be able to use them to follow the sequence of thought in an oral text.

Advanced-Plus   Able to understand the main ideas of most speech in a standard dialect; however, the listener may not be able to sustain comprehension in extended discourse which is propositionally and linguistically complex. Listener shows an emerging awareness of culturally implied meanings beyond the surface meanings of the text but may fail to grasp sociocultural nuances of the message.

Superior   The Superior level is characterized by an ability to understand concrete and abstract topics in extended discourse offered by speakers using native-like discourse strategies.

Superior   Able to understand the main ideas of all speech in a standard dialect, including technical discussion in a field of specialization. Can follow the essentials of extended discourse which is propositionally and linguistically complex, as in academic/professional settings, in lectures, speeches, and reports. Listener shows some appreciation of aesthetic norms of target language, of idioms, colloquialisms, and register shifting. Able to make inferences within the cultural framework of the target language. Understanding is aided by an awareness of the underlying organizational structure of the oral text and includes sensitivity for its social and cultural references and its affective overtones. Rarely misunderstands but may not understand excessively rapid, highly colloquial speech or speech that has strong cultural references.

Distinguished   The Distinguished level is characterized by an ability to understand accurately most linguistic styles and forms from within the cultural framework of the language.

Distinguished   Able to understand all forms and styles of speech pertinent to personal, social, and professional needs tailored to different audiences. Shows strong sensitivity to social and cultural references and aesthetic norms by processing language from within the cultural framework. Texts include theater plays, screen productions, editorials, symposia, academic debates, public policy statements, literary readings, and most jokes and puns. May have difficulty with some dialects and slang.

Generic Descriptions–Reading

These guidelines assume all reading texts to be authentic and legible.

Novice   The Novice level is characterized by an ability to
—identify isolated words and phrases when strongly supported by context; and
—identify learned material.

Novice-Low   Able occasionally to identify isolated words and/or major phrases when strongly supported by context.

Novice-Mid   Able to recognize the symbols of an alphabetic and/or syllabic writing system and/or a limited number of characters in a system that uses characters. The reader can identify an increasing number of highly contextualized words and/or phrases including cognates and borrowed words, where appropriate. Material understood rarely exceeds a single phrase at a time, and rereading may be required.

Novice-High   Has sufficient control of the writing system to interpret written language in areas of practical need. Where vocabulary has been learned, can read for instructional and directional purposes standardized messages, phrases, or expressions, such as some items on menus, schedules, timetables, maps, and signs. At times, but not on a consistent basis, the Novice-High-level reader may be able to derive meaning from material at a slightly higher level where context and/or extralinguistic background knowledge are supportive.

Intermediate   The Intermediate level is characterized by an ability to understand main ideas and some facts from simple connected texts.

Intermediate-Low   Able to understand main ideas and/or some facts from the simplest connected texts dealing with basic personal and social needs. Such texts are linguistically noncomplex and have a clear underlying internal structure, for example, chronological sequencing. They impart basic information about which the reader has to make only minimal suppositions or to which the reader brings personal interest and/or knowledge. Examples include messages with social purposes or information for the widest possible audience, such as public announcements and short, straightforward instructions dealing with public life. Some misunderstandings will occur.

Intermediate-Mid Able to read consistently with increased understanding simple connected texts dealing with a variety of basic and social needs. Such texts are still linguistically noncomplex and have a clear underlying internal structure. They impart basic information about which the reader has to make minimal suppositions and to which the reader brings personal interest and/or knowledge. Examples may include short, straightforward descriptions of persons, places, and things written for a wide audience.

Intermediate-High Able to read consistently with full understanding simple connected texts dealing with basic personal and social needs about which the reader has personal interest and/or knowledge. Can get some main ideas and information from texts at the next higher level featuring description and narration. Structural complexity may interfere with comprehension; for example, basic grammatical relations may be misinterpreted and temporal references may rely primarily on lexical items. Has some difficulty with the cohesive factors in discourse, such as matching pronouns with referents. While texts do not differ significantly from those at the Advanced level, comprehension is less consistent. May have to read material several times for understanding.

Advanced The Advanced level is characterized by
—an ability to read with consistent understanding prose several paragraphs in length, dealing primarily with factual information and intended for the general reader; and
—in areas of special interest or knowledge, an increasing ability to understand parts of texts which are propositionally and linguistically complex.

Advanced Able to read somewhat longer prose of several paragraphs in length, particularly if presented with a clear underlying structure. The prose is predominantly in familiar sentence patterns. Reader gets the main ideas and facts and misses some details. Comprehension derives not only from situational and subject-matter knowledge but also from increasing control of the language. Texts at this level include descriptions and narrations such as simple short stories, news items, bibliographical information, social notices, personal correspondence, routinized business letters, and simple technical material written for the general reader.

Advanced-Plus Able to follow essential points of written discourse at the Superior level in areas of special interest or knowledge. Able to understand parts of texts which are conceptually abstract and linguistically complex, and/or texts which treat unfamiliar topics and situations, as well as some texts which involve aspects of target-language culture. Able to comprehend the facts to make appropriate inferences. An emerging awareness of the aesthetic properties of language and of its literary styles permits comprehension of a wider variety of texts, including literary. Misunderstandings may occur.

Superior The Superior level is characterized by an ability to read, for information or for pleasure with almost complete comprehension and at normal speed, a wide variety of texts on a wide variety of topics.

Superior

Able to read with almost complete comprehension and at normal speed expository prose on unfamiliar subjects and a variety of literary texts. Reading ability is not dependent on subject-matter knowledge, although the reader is not expected to comprehend thoroughly texts which are highly dependent on knowledge of the target culture. Reads easily for pleasure. Superior-level texts feature hypotheses, argumentation, and supported opinions and include grammatical patterns and vocabulary ordinarily encountered in academic/professional reading. At this level, due to the control of general vocabulary and structure, the reader is almost always able to match the meanings derived from extralinguistic knowledge with meanings derived from knowledge of the language, allowing for smooth and efficient reading of diverse texts. Occasional misunderstandings may still occur; for example, the reader may experience some difficulty with unusually complex structures and low-frequency idioms. At the Superior level the reader can match strategies, top-down or bottom-up, which are most appropriate to the text. (Top-down strategies rely on real-world knowledge and prediction based on genre and organizational scheme of the text. Bottom-up strategies rely on actual linguistic knowledge.) Material at this level will include a variety of literary texts, editorials, correspondence, general reports, and technical material in professional fields. Rereading is rarely necessary, and misreading is rare.

Distinguished

The Distinguished level is characterized by an ability to read fluently and accurately most styles and forms of the language with comprehension that is achieved from within the cultural framework of the language and that includes appreciation of nuance and subtlety.

Distinguished

Able to read fluently and accurately most styles and forms of the language pertinent to academic and professional needs. Able to relate inferences in the text to real-world knowledge and understand almost all sociolinguistic and cultural references by processing language from within the cultural framework. Able to understand a writer's use of nuance and subtlety. Can readily follow unpredictable turns of thought and author intent in such materials as sophisticated editorials, specialized journal articles, and literary texts such as novels, plays, poems, as well as in any subject-matter area directed to the general reader.

Generic Descriptions–Writing

Novice

The Novice level is characterized by an ability to produce isolated words and phrases.

Novice-Low

Able to form some letters in an alphabetic system. In languages whose writing systems use syllabaries or characters, writer is able to both copy and produce the basic strokes. Can produce romanization of isolated characters, where applicable.

Novice-Mid

Able to copy or transcribe familiar words or phrases and reproduce some from memory. No practical communicative writing skills.

Novice-High

Able to write simple fixed expressions and limited memorized material and some recombinations thereof. Can supply information on simple forms and documents. Can write names, numbers, dates, own nationality, and other simple autobiographical information, as well as some short phrases and simple lists. Can write all the symbols in an alphabetic or syllabic system or 50–100 characters or compounds in a character writing system. Spelling and representation of symbols (letters, syllables, characters) may be partially correct.

Intermediate   The Intermediate level is characterized by an ability to meet practical writing needs by communicating simple facts and ideas in a loose collection of sentences.

Intermediate-Low   Able to meet limited practical writing needs. Can write short messages, postcards, and take down simple notes, such as telephone messages. Can create statements or questions within the scope of limited language experience. Material produced consists of recombinations of learned vocabulary and structures into simple sentences on very familiar topics. Language is inadequate to express in writing anything but elementary needs. Frequent errors in grammar, vocabulary, punctuation, spelling, and in formation of nonalphabetic symbols, but writing can be understood by natives used to the writing of nonnatives.

Intermediate-Mid   Able to meet a number of practical writing needs. Can write short, simple letters. Content involves personal preferences, daily routine, everyday events, and other topics grounded in personal experience. Can express present time or at least one other time frame or aspect consistently, e.g., nonpast, habitual, imperfective. Evidence of control of the syntax of noncomplex sentences and basic inflectional morphology, such as declensions and conjugation. Writing tends to be a loose collection of sentences or sentence fragments on a given topic and provides little evidence of conscious organization. Can be understood by natives used to the writing of nonnatives.

Intermediate-High   Able to meet most practical writing needs and limited social demands. Can take notes in some detail on familiar topics and respond in writing to personal questions. Can write simple letters, brief synopses and paraphrases, summaries of biographical data, work and school experience. In those languages relying primarily on content words and time expressions to express time, tense, or aspect, some precision is displayed; where tense and/or aspect is expressed through verbal inflection, forms are produced rather consistently, but not always accurately. An ability to describe and narrate in paragraphs is emerging. Rarely uses basic cohesive elements, such as pronominal substitutions or synonyms in written discourse. Writing, though faulty, is generally comprehensible to natives used to the writing of nonnatives.

Advanced   The Advanced level is characterized by an ability to write narratives and descriptions of a factual nature of at least several paragraphs in length on familiar topics.

Advanced   Able to write routine social correspondence and join sentences in simple discourse of at least several paragraphs in length on familiar topics. Can write simple social correspondence, take notes, write cohesive summaries and resumes, as well as narratives and descriptions of a factual nature. Has sufficient writing vocabulary to express self simply with some circumlocution. May still make errors in punctuation, spelling, or the formation of nonalphabetic symbols. Good control of the morphology and the most frequently used syntactic structures, e.g., common word order patterns, coordination, subordination, but makes frequent errors in producing complex sentences. Uses a limited number of cohesive devices, such as pronouns, accurately. Writing may resemble literal translations from the native language, but a sense of organization (rhetorical structure) is emerging. Writing is understandable to natives not used to the writing of nonnatives.

Advanced-Plus
Able to write about a variety of topics with significant precision and in detail. Can write most social and informal business correspondence. Can describe and narrate personal experiences fully but has difficulty supporting points of view in written discourse. Can write about the concrete aspects of topics relating to particular interests and special fields of competence. Often shows remarkable fluency and ease of expression, but under time constraints and pressure writing may be inaccurate. Generally strong in either grammar or vocabulary, but not in both. Weakness and unevenness in one of the foregoing or in spelling or character writing formation may result in occasional miscommunication. Some misuse of vocabulary may still be evident. Style may still be obviously foreign.

Superior
The Superior level is characterized by an ability to write formally and informally on practical, social, and professional topics.

Superior
Able to express self effectively in most formal and informal writing on practical, social, and professional topics. Can write most types of correspondence, such as memos as well as social and business letters, and short research papers and statements of position in areas of special interest or in special fields. Good control of a full range of structures, spelling or nonalphabetic symbol production, and a wide general vocabulary allow the writer to hypothesize and present arguments or points of view accurately and effectively. An underlying organization, such as chronological ordering, logical ordering, cause and effect, comparison, and thematic development is strongly evident, although not thoroughly executed and/or not totally reflecting target-language patterns. Although sensitive to differences in formal and informal style, still may not tailor writing precisely to a variety of purposes and/or readers. Errors in writing rarely disturb natives or cause miscommunication.

2

From Defining to Developing Proficiency: A Look at the Decisions

Vicki Galloway
*American Council on the
Teaching of Foreign Languages*

In any educational endeavor, according to Alfred North Whitehead, a stage of enthusiasm or "romance" must always precede a stage of precision. This stage of romance is one characterized by novelty, excitement, ferment, which gives forth "unexplored connections with possibilities . . . of wide significance . . . half disclosed, half concealed" (50, p. 17). For some educators, this stage of romance is an extravagance—costly, time-consuming, and inefficient for themselves and their students. For other educators, this stage of romance is neverending and inescapable; it merely shifts periodically from one topic or idea to another. But enthusiasm without scrutiny, analysis, and systematization is deceptively euphoric, and precision without romance is barren and inert. One without the other is not progress. It may be said that "proficiency" is in its romance epoch.

Certainly there is nothing new about the goal of proficiency. It is a word which language educators have used for years, often interchangeably with such descriptors as *good, fluent, knowledgeable, bilingual,* and *competent.* Although never really stated, it has often carried a sense of some ultimate, if somewhat mythical and mysterious, end—a point at which one becomes "able," at which one's work is "finished." The finality of the phenomenon has also been conveyed by a lack of necessity for qualification:

Vicki Galloway (Ph.D., University of South Carolina) is Project Director at ACTFL and Editor of *Foreign Language Annals.* She served for six years as State Supervisor of Foreign Languages and International Studies for South Carolina and has taught foreign language at both secondary and college levels. She has published in the *Modern Language Journal, Northeast Conference Reports,* and ACTFL Foreign Language Education Series and has conducted workshops on various aspects of foreign language education at all levels of instruction.

"he's proficient in French" has rarely occasioned the responses, "how proficient?" or "proficient at what?"

The ACTFL Proficiency Guidelines represent the combined efforts of groups of educators to provide an operational definition for this long-elusive term, to represent it as phenomena observable and evolving. In this sense, the guidelines pose to the profession a construct for examining and ultimately assessing the extraclassroom behaviors of language learners.

The enthusiasm with which the guidelines have been greeted is undeniable. It is also natural and, if one agrees with Whitehead, necessary. But enthusiasm is not without its dangers. New ideas and procedures are easily subject to the pitfalls of popularity. Stevenson (6) cautions against the loss of a "spirit of validation," alluding to a chain of events such as the one loosely captured in the following scenario:

> There is an air of need, a vacuum. Something comes along to fill this need. The need is so intense that the new object gains immediate acceptance. The object seems to "work." Needs are satisfied and the object remains unquestioned. Expectations are high and thus the object is misused, stretched beyond its original purpose. Functional scepticism yields to the fervor of bandwagon behavior.

It is essential that the appropriate climate be maintained for the future validation and application of the proficiency concept, that its limitations and potential be explored, that discussion arise from knowledge and understanding of the concepts presented for scrutiny, and that impatience for facts not preclude the consideration of speculation and approximation. The guidelines, as presented in revised form in this volume, presume no final answers, rather, they reflect a refusal of paralysis in the search for the right questions.

One of the most appropriate, most interesting, yet most difficult questions is the following: presuming that proficiency is measurable and that the guidelines have captured an approximate construct of the phenomenon, how can proficiency be produced in the foreign language classroom? While it is always risky to draw conclusions from product to process, clearly there is room for speculation which draws not from feature-specific information as contained in the guidelines, but rather from a sense of the nature of the concept and the developmental scheme which the definitions represent. Since the guidelines present neither a curricular model nor a methodological prescription, attempts at direct application of surface-level criteria to instructional planning and implementation will likely result in the trivialization of learning experiences and the loss of program direction. Indeed, curricular *application* of the level descriptions is destined to be *misapplication* for three reasons. First, the word *apply* connotes purpose and particular use, and the purpose and particular use of the level descriptions as contained in the revised guidelines is assessment. Second, the word *apply* brings the sense of superimposing, covering, as with new paint to old walls—that is, of changing the outward appearance, not the inner nature. Third, *to apply* means to bring into action. Yet, the level descriptions contained in this volume are, in appearance, quite lifeless, seemingly composed of discrete-looking behaviors. What should be sought from the guidelines in terms of curriculum and instruction is not *applications,* but *implications.* It is only by looking under the surface level that the dynamic nature of proficiency is exposed. The real nonassessment potential of the guidelines lies in capturing these undercurrents and in deriving from them a sense of the types of decisions that must be made in planning and implementing instruction for classroom learners. The purpose of this chapter is to review and synthesize the concepts underlying the proposed proficiency assessment framework, to address limitations to their applicability, and to extract from these more global notions possible implications for efforts in the areas of curriculum and instruction.

The Nature of the Guidelines

The concept of proficiency, as represented in the ACTFL guidelines, is often referred to in terms of a progression or continuum. It is described this way in order to stress two fundamental characteristics. First, proficiency is not defined as a series of discrete-point equidistant steps or as a system with broad leaps and underlying gaps. Rather, as a representation of communicative growth, the levels describe a hierarchical sequence of performance ranges. Second, each level of proficiency subsumes all previous levels in a kind of "all before and more" system so that succeeding levels are characterized both by overlap and refinement.

The more closely the phenomenon of proficiency is examined, however, the less it resembles a linear progression and the more it resembles an outward spiral, representational of an individual's expanding access to the target language environment. In the core of this spiral is the individual whose linguistic proficiency (or lack of it) allows only tourist-level access to a somewhat neutral and neutralized environment where native speakers cater to his demands, adjust to his communicative level, and somehow extract meaning from his utterances. As linguistic proficiency increases, this individual is afforded greater opportunity to interact in more and varied personal, social, and professional contexts. As he moves out of the neutral core, he assumes proportionately more of the burden of message transmission, since less of this burden must fall on his interlocutor. Along with increasing interactive contexts, then, come greater expectations on the part of interlocutors, both linguistically and culturally. While this naive illustration does not presume to account for the complexities of language learning and proficiency development, it can serve to disabuse the notion of a point-and-line scale having a distinct beginning and end.

Further, it allows for the visualization of learner progress not in terms of framed stages, but in terms of *rhythms* in which language use is "there and evolving." Proficiency as depicted through this model, then, deals not with one's knowledge of grammar or simply with one's ability to get a message across, but with one's ability to function effectively in real life. Simply asking whether or not an individual is communicating will not allow us to locate his or her position on the performance spiral. Instead, four questions must be asked:

Why?	=	Function
What?	=	Content
Where?	=	Context
How (well)?	=	Accuracy

Through a spiral representation of proficiency, the inisolable nature of these components is more vividly demonstrated. Each of the level narratives of the proficiency guidelines focuses on responding to the above questions, thus presenting a performance profile of the individual in terms of functions or tasks that can be performed, types of content or contexts in which they can be performed, and a description of the range of accuracy with which language will be received or produced. Every level represents a "new constellation of interrelationships" (Higgs, 22) between these criteria: function, content/context, and accuracy.

While conceptually these components may hold interesting implications for classroom instruction and curriculum development, their nomenclature can serve to constrain the interpretive possibilities and result in serious misapplication. The labels of *function, content/context,* and *accuracy* are unfortunate for three primary reasons. First they tend to produce discrete associations and result in oversimplified or erroneous equations—e.g., *accuracy* = number of mistakes or *content* = amount of vocabulary. Second, the labeling of components produces their artificial separation and fails to capture their interactive and interdependent qualities. Third, while such terminology may be useful in discussions of productive skills, it transfers only inadequately to hypothesized receptive skills constructs. Yet, each of these components encompasses communicative decision-making continua not directly observable through the shorthand of the guidelines themselves. It is through these continua that the framework of proficiency constructs itself. As a prelude to discussion of curricular and instructional implications, then, this section will present an overview of the components in terms of their more global underlying concepts, with the purpose of conveying a sense of the ranges of the various factors involved in proficiency. The now-familiar speaking guidelines will be examined first, followed, for comparison, by an unweaving of the revised reading guidelines. It should be noted that the components—context/content, function, and accuracy—are separated here merely for the purpose of observation; an awareness of their interactional nature is crucial to an understanding of proficiency as defined through the ACTFL guidelines.

The Speaking Guidelines

Context and Content. The term *context* refers to the various situations in which an individual uses the language. The guidelines do not enumerate specific situations for each level, but they do indicate a hierarchical arrangement based on the amount and type of interaction (Byrnes, this volume) generally required by a given range of situation types. Certainly, in isolation of other factors, situations themselves bear no inherent difficulty ranking. Yet, as the amount and variety of interaction increase, so do the options for defining and approaching the communicative situation, thus increasing the demands for flexibility placed on the user and decreasing the direct applicability of learned or memorized utterances. In this sense, contexts in which the individual meets rudimentary social and physical needs will likely provide more definite and predictable conversational parameters in which one's speech may be guided by interlocutor prompting through natural use of unrequested repetitions, frequent comprehension checks, multiple descriptions, and other clarification devices. Thus, context continua, as represented below, progress from the more reactive, familiar, discrete, and predictable ranges of situations to those which require greater degrees of integration and speaker control and less dependence on fixed and predictable transactional maps.

Context

noninitiating ....initiating
familiar ....unfamiliar
discrete...integrative
predictable ....unpredictable

The term *content* refers to the types and ranges of topics addressed through conversation. As illustrated below, the guidelines represent appropriateness of topic at each level through three continua, which pass from immediate, autobiographical, factual, and concrete (transparent referents) to topics more abstract, esoteric, and remote in time and place. An underlying quality is captured in the "detachment/investment" continuum which considers the degree of personal involvement and risk-taking demanded of the speaker by the topic. For American students, subjects such as family, work, school, and hobbies, for example, provide a relatively lower risk factor than "issues" topics which expose speaker knowledge, opinion, and evaluation. Investment here should not be confused with the word *involvement,* since willingness to interact on a given topic is a requisite for communicating at any level. Rather, investment refers to the degree to which the topic range is likely to require greater recourse to one's own identity with the attendant risk of greater loss of face. This continuum thus reflects the learner's gradual shift from thinking about language form to thinking *in* the language in order to convey messages and to present one's self through these messages.

Content

detachment	investment
concrete	abstract
immediate	distant

Function. The term *function* refers to what the user does with the language. As used in the proficiency guidelines, it bears neither the specificity nor the distinct purpose orientation of that used in discussions of functional-notional syllabus design. Rather, functions here are global components, more properly thought of as task universals or categories.

Function is perhaps the most crucial element in oral proficiency assessment. If the speaker cannot combine linguistic resources to perform communicative tasks, explicit knowledge of grammar and vocabulary is of questionable value. The following continua of task ranges are roughly represented through the oral proficiency progression:

Function

transact	negotiate
state	support
identify	describe
enumerate	narrate
inform	conjecture

This hierarchical arrangement reflects not only the amount and variety of interaction but also the cognitive and linguistic demands triggered by a given task range. The continua thus progress (1) from the performance of clear-cut transactional tasks to those demanding higher flexibility, requiring the speaker to "sense" or "read" the situation and adjust task performance accordingly; (2) from stating an opinion to providing cohesive and coherent arguments in support of that opinion; (3) from identification of discrete elements to the sensorial richness and explicitness of description; (4) from listing occurrences to telling the story—meshing the descriptive background with the sequential recounting of events in past, present, or future time frame; and (5) from the level of information provision to that of hypothesis formation, where one enters the world of conjecture, of "freely arranging and interrelating abstract concepts and real-life entities to make new realities" (Byrnes, 7, p. 195). It should be noted, however, that despite the centrality of these functions or task types, the manner in which and the extent to which they are carried out is a result of their interaction with the other components—content/context and accuracy. Greater sophistication in the performance of a given function will be a product of the topic and situation, as well as the degree of precision in meeting the performance parameters demanded by both.

Accuracy. Of all the components, accuracy holds the greatest potential for misinterpretation since it refers not to the traditional classroom sense of "number of mistakes" but to a host of factors that, with a given situation, topic, and task, respond to the questions "how" and "how well." A predominant consideration in the speaking progression is the fidelity of message transmission and reception. Recognizing the virtual impossibility of absolute correspondence between message sent and message received, it would seem that the more appropriate, acceptable, and precise the linguistic packaging, the greater the level of confidence for transmitting the speaker's intentions.

While occasional mistakes may not produce breakdowns in communication, patterns of errors and repeated misuse of lexical, structural, or syntactic elements may (Galloway, 18). The guidelines for speaking thus presume a strong relationship between communicative success and grammatical accuracy in which "grammar" denotes the *meaning access system.*

Accuracy

    deliberate..automatic
    patterned ....flexible
    telegraphic/holophrastic.....................extended discourse
    global/general ....explicit, precise
    frequent error patterns ....infrequent, unpatterned error
    inappropriateness..............................appropriateness
    sympathetic listener...........................nonsympathetic listener

The first two continua denote the extent to which the language user is controlled by or in control of the language—from deliberate and conscious attention to form to automatic reliance on routinized underlying skills, and thus to the freedom and tactical use afforded by increased internalization of the linguistic code. This range describes the extent to which the learner's use of the language has reached what Whitehead refers to as the "stage of generalizations" (50, p. 19):

The stage of shedding details in favour of the active application of principles, the details retreating into subconscious habits. We don't go about explicitly retaining in our own minds that two and two make four, though once we had to learn it by heart. The essence of this stage is the emergence from the comparative passivity of being trained into the active freedom of application.

Conversely, the speaker's lack of flexibility and of well-developed message formation will likely place a burden on the listener: the one-word utterance will be subject to varying interpretations; the patterned repertoire will result in the forced fit of message/intent. Both will leave the listener to frame the message, while the cohesion and developmental features of discourse will serve to lessen the guessing factor of the interlocutor. Thus, the degree of speaker reliance on the interlocutor constitutes one factor in accuracy assessment and reflects the need for linguistically sympathetic listeners during speakers' varied transitional interlanguage stages. As Higgs (21, p. 290) notes, "ill-formed communicative tokens succeed *only* when listeners assume a communicative intent on the part of the nonnative and implicitly accept a disproportionate share of the communicative burden."

The Reading Guidelines

In contrast to the productive skills, the guidelines' progression for receptive skills assessment reverses, to some extent, the communicative role from that of creating utterances to that of receiving them. However, to view any of the skills at this level alone would be to reduce the communicative process to a series of stimulus-response, catch-and-throw rituals. As Byrnes (8) points out, the categories *receptive* and *productive* are merely artificial classifiers for, whether speaker, writer, listener, or reader, one produces meaning.

As noted earlier, the labels used to identify the various components of the speaking skills become less illustrative and useful when applied to the reading skills. Yet, as both are interactive processes, it is possible to identify and classify nearly complementary sets of performance continua in the reading skills. Since the written message is the vehicle through which both participants—originator and responder—are joined, proficiency assessment criteria, as represented in the ACTFL guidelines, reflect a text-driven system.

The following discussion extracts components from the reading proficiency guidelines for the purpose of display grouping. Yet, as was earlier noted, the components are not isolable but rather in constant interplay.

Context and Content. The previous discussion of context in terms of oral proficiency highlighted several key considerations: first, that context refers to situation; second, that some situations may present the language user with more predictable conversational parameters than others; and third, that the more varied and extensive the interaction becomes, the more the speaker must collect from his linguistic and extralinguistic arsenal. These same considerations might be applied to a discussion of context in the reading skills where again the factors of predictability, familiarity, and degree of integration demanded come into play. In short, the guidelines reflect the assumption that what the reader brings to the text, what is stored in terms of nonlinguistic experiences, or knowledge, will influence the message the reader produces from the text.

The following continua might be constructed to reflect the situational expectations with which readers approach a given text:

Context

situation conformity ....situation nonconformity
genre conformity....................................genre nonconformity
experience accessibility..........................experience inaccessibility
target culture inaccessibility ....target culture accessibility

As one component of reading proficiency, this group of continua constitutes the environmental expansion factor discussed at the beginning of this chapter. Readers at the lower levels of the proficiency scale will require texts which, either alone or supplemented by some extratextual apparatus, allow some check on the interpretive options available and fit within the readers' broad cultural, experiential, and knowledge frameworks. As represented by this group of continua, one aspect of a reader's proficiency would thus involve the amount and type of relevant information the reader is able to feed into the text in order to decrease his distance from the author's frame of reference. Educators have stressed the importance of this shared information factor and the extent to which its absence can produce creative misunderstandings as the reader seeks to validate his own experience-based predictions.

Content, or topic selection of a text, takes into consideration criteria similar to those outlined in the oral proficiency continua: the degree of transparency or extent to which the topic is one to which the reader can directly relate; the topic's immediacy—whether it lies within the realm of general public consumption or in more esoteric and specialized domains. A further dimension, that of passage density, relates to the proportion of concepts or information in the passage to the overall length of the passage (Kaya-Carton and Carton, 27). Higher density passages would contain many concepts expressed in a very concise manner and therefore might be expected to produce greater demands on the reader.

Content

general audience..specialized audience
transparency/directness ....opacity/indirectness
familiarity..nonfamiliarity
low density ....high density

Accuracy. In the previous discussion of oral proficiency, the accuracy component was essentially divided into three aspects: (1) the degree of communicative precision, (2) the degree of speaker flexibility, and (3) the degree of dependence on the interlocutor.

Applied to the domain of written message reception, the first two communicative criteria relate the extent to which and the efficiency with which authentic reading acts are realized. The first of these translates into fidelity of comprehension in meeting reader purpose or author intent. The second criterion concerns speed—the amount of text-involvement time required for the reader to fulfill the designated purpose.

Accuracy

frequent misunderstanding................infrequent misunderstanding
halting ....fluent
context-embedded..............................context-reduced
recurrence, exemplification ....assumption, subtlety
explicit text organizers ....implicit text organizers
conventional......................................idiosyncratic
linguistic simplicity...........................linguistic intricacy
nonambiguous....................................ambiguous

The third criterion of accuracy—dependence on interlocutor—when applied to reading skills, factors out several continua, a grouping characterized by features of textuality. Although these features would not commonly be construed as corresponding to an accuracy component, they do address the receiver's linguistic dependence on the sender. Contained, therefore, in this series of continua are factors involving the manner in which the author develops a message and identifies and approaches the readership. In all cases, unflawed texts must be assumed to the extent possible.

At the earliest levels, the written word is couched in some nonambiguous environmental context which lies outside the language of the text and allows for reader dependence on situational referents or physical cues. Cummins (14, p. 120) refers to the extremes in range of contextual support available for receiving meaning as "embedded" and "reduced." The former allows participants' reliance on familiar and shared situational cues, whereas the latter derives from reliance on linguistic cues to meaning where a shared reality cannot be assumed. Texts at the lower end of the range may also contain frequent exemplification, redundancy, repetition of thought through rephrasing and summation. Further, while beginning readers may rely heavily on visual and direct text organizers such as bold print, subheadings, and the like, the more proficient reader will access and utilize implicit organizers which are more propositional in nature. The linguistic complexity range refers to such aspects as syntactic variety, use of idiomatic or highly colloquial language, as well as to length and punctuation patterns. Kaya-Carton and Carton (27) note an additional factor correlated with increased reading proficiency—that is, the degree of "noise" or ambiguity which may interfere with comprehension. "Noisy" passages are those that include irrelevant information or lend themselves to a variety of interpretations and thus will require a higher degree of tolerance from readers seeking to comprehend them.

Function. In examining what the reader does with a given text—i.e., what tasks are performed—it is tempting to think in terms of reader strategies such as skimming, scanning, gisting, sorting, and so forth. However, the revised ACTFL guidelines, as assessment criteria, purposely reflect a product rather than a process orientation. While the reader's efficient use of task-appropriate strategies will likely have bearing on the accuracy criteria, these strategies constitute performance routes, rather than performance of communicative tasks themselves. In terms of function, therefore, one continuum can be established:

Function

recognition ....comprehension

Here, comprehension refers to carrying out tasks that lie within the realm of author-intended purpose. Defined in this way, the function component may only be identified through its interaction with other components which establish the circle of author intent as well as expectation parameters for authentic reader purposes within this realm. The following continuum thus reflects ranges of communicative intent of participants originating and responding to texts (Child, this volume):

orientational/instructional...............................evaluative/projective

Child refers to this as a "mode" range, where *mode* refers to the way or manner in which texts can be judged according to their evident purposes. This text range proceeds from the lower levels which orient "all concerned regarding who or what is where and what is happening or supposed to happen" and those which convey information about real-world occurrences or existing objects and events. At the upper end of the continuum are those texts which range from analysis and evaluation of shared background events to the highly individualized, culture-bound texts in which "shared information and assumptions are at a minimum and personal input is paramount." (See Child, this volume.) Implicit in this continuum is once again the risk-taking factor, as reader purposes lying within these author intent domains will proceed from those with lower reader self-investment to those demanding increasingly greater exposure of self through evaluation and projection.

This section has examined the various interactive components of proficiency in terms of underlying progressions in order to capture a sense of the dynamic nature of the performance criteria implicit in the ACTFL guidelines. The purpose has been to elucidate not the immediate level-to-level criteria as contained in the guidelines but rather to convey a more global picture of the destination ranges which can be derived from the discrete descriptors. The following section will draw from these insights and from the more global scheme of the guidelines as they are used for proficiency assessment with the purpose of drawing implications for curriculum and instruction.

Implications of the Guidelines for Curriculum and Instruction

Drawing practical implications from a conceptual framework is fraught with difficulty for, as there exist neither the sturdy bridges nor the reliable stepping-stones of research to join the two, one must make a speculative leap. The process of extracting and interpreting principles from the proficiency guidelines is admittedly one of selective observation, subject to the stretch and shrink of one's own bias. It is a process destined to produce only "maybe's," all of which will receive their share of accord and dissent. It is therefore hoped that no "prescription for proficiency" will be construed from the various notions presented here, but rather that the discussion may serve as a springboard for examining the relative effectiveness of current practices. Clearly, the roads to proficiency are as many and varied as are the descriptions of the destinations themselves.

In this section, three general characteristics of the ACTFL Proficiency Guidelines will be used to organize discussion and catalyze thought on the issues of teaching for proficiency. Each of these statements relates to a fundamental aspect of proficiency as defined by the ACTFL guidelines:

in terms of what is observed
1. The guidelines describe levels of proficiency in four skills in terms of performance of real-life functions in ever-expanding personal, social, and professional contexts;

in terms of how it is determined
2. An assessment of proficiency indicates the highest observed level of sustained performance of an individual;

and in terms of with whom it is demonstrated
3. The guidelines contain references to the interlocutor.

1. THE GUIDELINES DESCRIBE LEVELS OF PROFICIENCY IN FOUR SKILLS IN TERMS OF THE PERFORMANCE OF REAL-LIFE FUNCTIONS IN EVER-EXPANDING PERSONAL, SOCIAL, AND PROFESSIONAL CONTEXTS.

Proficiency, as described through the ACTFL guidelines, is concerned with observable behavior, with what an individual does in the language. It deals not with separate and weighted examinations of explicit rules, but rather with the extent to which knowledge of the target language system, explicit or implicit, can be applied to language use. It refers not to prepared and rehearsed activity, nor is it defined through peer-relative measures of mastery of particular course content. Instead, proficiency considers the extent to which an individual can combine linguistic and extralinguistic resources for spontaneous communication in unpredictable contexts free from the insistent prompts and prodding of the classroom. This curriculum-free nature of the proficiency guidelines limits their direct transportability to curriculum and instruction either as learner goal statements or as learner achievement indicators.

The proficiency guidelines are written to provide a global sense of learner performance expectancies at various positioned stages of evolution. Although the criteria for each level set somewhat strict parameters as to what constitutes level-characteristic behavior, these criteria represent not discrete behaviors, but performance ranges as observed in learner profiles that are highly individual and varied. As assessment criteria, the level descriptions at times focus less on what the individual *does* and more on what the individual *does not do yet.* In extracurricular performance assessment, such distinctions are crucial, for they establish the accuracy parameters in reference to certain communicative tasks and thus serve to hold level expectations in check. However, because of this focus on deficiencies, the guidelines are inadequate as program goal statements. In the world of the classroom, one does not work toward a negative destination nor, if the destination is realizable, does one strive to get only part of the way there. In the world of the classroom, realistic goals are operationalized through the more specific outcome statements which drive course content, and "accuracy" denotes the extent to which outcomes are achieved. *Course outcomes are assessed only through achievement testing,* and if these course outcomes are expressed in terms of a learner's performance in using the language, as they would be in a proficiency-based curriculum, then achievement tests will measure that performance.

Because of their extracurricular nature, the descriptions contained in the guidelines say nothing about the time or effort involved in reaching a level or the length of time likely to be spent at any given level.

Therefore, the question "Where should my students be at the end of X semesters (or years) of language study?"—albeit an interesting and legitimate one—is unanswerable through the guidelines themselves. The time required to reach a stated level of proficiency will vary according to the skill area, the individual, the language, the instructional program, and perhaps a host of other factors. These considerations prompt caution in the use of proficiency ratings for placement and entrance and exit criteria. Their use as a placement device would seem feasible only in conjunction with a functional performance-based curriculum whose level-to-level goals are clearly defined and articulated and whose objectives would capture the on-level performance ranges of an individual and provide for growth. Likewise, the establishment of an arbitrary, absolute, and noncompensatory proficiency requirement in a given skill would seem inadvisable. The myriad variations of individual performance, as well as the limits to instructional control over that performance, counsel the establishment of minimum standards only through careful and studied data collection and curricular examination, and caution against a one-skill, one-measure indication of learner language ability. Second, the length of time spent at a given level will vary. Although relatively rapid progress may be made through the Novice level, Heilenman and Kaplan (20) note that in the speaking skills the intermediate level is a notorious plateau period, during which progress seems minimal even when effort is maximal. Lowe (33) and Véguez (49) cite the occasional intransigence of the Advanced/Advanced Plus speaker, the latter alluding to the need for more diagnostic-based instruction at this level to determine individual needs profiles and to gear instruction accordingly.

The guidelines do not clearly display small increments of learning. They are useful in providing perspective and a global sense of the learner's progression which can be drawn upon in preparing instructional goal statements. Indeed, as Heilenman and Kaplan (20) note, perhaps the greatest contribution of the guidelines is that they restore validity to the concept of the apprentice language user. In this sense they have great potential for curbing the notoriously unrealistic expectations that teachers have had for students and that students have had for their instruction and for themselves. Yet, the guidelines themselves must stand apart from curriculum, with proficiency assessment, at this stage, serving most usefully in a program evaluation capacity. Thus, the proficiency progression cannot be viewed as the steady and uniform movement of identically packaged language learners along a conveyor belt. Proficiency-based course and program goals should reflect realistic experience-based expectations and be able to accommodate level-to-level overlap so that progress can be measured even during plateau periods. Program objectives should recognize not simply gross or obvious periods of communicative growth, but the subtler, yet necessary, ones as well.

Four Skills

It is unfortunate that the concept of "proficiency" has of late been coupled so tenaciously with speaking skills, as if one communicative channel held some inherent superiority, some greater worth, or some mysterious potential as an overall indicator of language ability. Yet, the reasons for this lopsided focus should be fairly clear. First, it is the product of a 25-year tradition, the result of language teaching's rather painful divorce from a grammar-translation marriage. As the espousal of the goal of communication, and especially communicative competence, began reaching the classroom teacher in the post-audiolingual seventies, it became heavily linked with oral expression. The words *use the language,* contained in shorthand definitions of communicative competence, held strong associations with utterance production for many classroom teachers. Further, the incipient development of these communicative skills was visible, therefore rewarding; and teachers, once having built up an error tolerance level, could witness interaction taking place. In survey after survey, nine out of ten students stated their first priority as "speak the language." In textbooks, and even in the professional literature, the disparaging skill classifiers "passive" and "active" are experiencing a very slow death.

The advent of academic oral proficiency assessment procedures has intensified this focus, for in the story of education, what is measured exists and what is not, does not (the rationale for ACTFL's initial oral proficiency assessment efforts is chronicled elsewhere in this volume, as are the efforts underway to develop assessment instruments in the receptive skills). But oral skills are only one communicative modality. Richards (40) states: "Language proficiency is . . . not a global factor but can only be defined with reference to particular performance skills and behaviors in specialized language modalities." The ACTFL guidelines present progressions in four modalities and, as revised, attempt to account for the uniqueness of each. A strong implication of this acknowledgment is the need to examine goals and objectives, first for the extent to which they reflect learner and institutional priorities in skill development and second, for the extent to which they represent a developmental scheme which considers the unique properties and characteristics of each of these four skills and articulates learner preparedness. Rarely would a self-respecting language textbook or teacher end a discussion of foreign language methods without mentioning at some point a "four-skills approach." In practice, however, one might question how the four skills are approached, whether in some cases they do not serve as the merest pretext for the analysis of grammar or whether the one skill actually nurtured is not the drill skill. A far too real scenario is evoked by the student who rises from the ranks of basal-level instruction, steps fitfully across the bridge of the conversation and/or composition course, and enters the "upper division"—a place where one reads literature whether or not one has learned to read.

Perhaps a tacit assumption underlying the above practices is that proficiency can be equated with some factor, such as knowledge of grammar. Yet, the proficiency progressions as outlined in the ACTFL guidelines highlight the various contributory factors of each of the four skills, thus capturing at the very least a sense of what proficiency is not. In speaking, for example, it becomes clear that proficiency is not simply a knowledge of grammar rules nor simply the ability to "substitute the indefinite determiner for the possessive determiner in the following sentences." Further, sources of difficulty in reading comprehension are likely to be the content, as well as the language. Thus, two primary questions arise in the examination of classroom activities: (1) is the activity geared to the development of a usable skill, and does it reflect the nature of that skill domain; and (2) what is the real purpose of the activity—does it develop what it purports to develop? In short, are so-called "speaking" or "conversatión" activities serving merely as error exposure devices; is a reading passage serving as little more than a lexical supply for an ensuing question-and-answer routine?

Richards (40) notes that just as proficiency as observed behavior cannot be accounted for by any single unitary underlying ability, proficiency in one modality does not imply proficiency in other modalities. It should not be assumed that at any point in time an individual will be at the same level of proficiency across the four skills. On the contrary, educators have, of late, been focusing on a "decoupling" of the receptive and productive skills. The concept of a "comprehension advantage" posited by Stevick (47), among others, holds that people are generally able to understand more than they are able to produce and much more than they are able to produce correctly. This hypothesis, widely accepted by the language teaching community, contends that for nonnative speakers, listening and reading comprehension will exceed speaking by some measurable amount.

Research conducted at government language schools reveals some interesting data in this regard and indicates that in the listening skills this degree of "offset" may well vary according to the language. Lowe (33) reports that test results from learners of Spanish revealed higher scores in listening than in speaking in 76 percent of the cases. This discrepancy was strongest at the more advanced levels where the amount of offset was as great as two full levels on the ILR scale [e.g., a speaker at the advanced level (ILR 2) was able to understand at level 4]. Interestingly enough, the discrepancy was nonexistent for Spanish learners at the Novice and Intermediate ranges: at levels Intermediate-High and lower, listening comprehension and speaking scores were equal. In French, however, listening comprehension scores were higher than speaking scores only 47 percent of the time, and the range of discrepancy was much smaller, approximately one ILR level. Yet, the positive offset was displayed in French much earlier than in the Spanish group, occurring at the Novice-High to Intermediate levels. Lowe hypothesizes that in some languages—such as Vietnamese, Thai, Japanese, Korean, Chinese, and Arabic—an actual negative offset might exist; that is, listening comprehension may be lower than speaking proficiency, due perhaps to such factors as tonality, sociocultural elements, dialect variation, and lack of recognizable cognates. The revised ACTFL guidelines in the receptive skills recognize the possibility for a positive offset by the addition of a "distinguished" performance range beyond that of "superior."

Conclusive evidence of the existence of this "comprehension advantage" across languages and across levels, such as that provided by validated receptive skills proficiency measures, would prove helpful in goal setting and course-content planning. While the concept already enjoys widespread acceptance, the possibilities for a dominant skills contagion effect have not been fully explored. If reading and listening, for example, show this positive offset, it seems feasible that through carefully designed curricula and materials these skills can be "hooked into" and serve to pull up other skills as well. Surely, while each skill should be nurtured within the learner's own developmental scheme, the possibilities for skill exploitation should not be overlooked.

While oral proficiency may long continue to be the goal to which language learners aspire, an oral-skills-only approach to language instruction may militate against the learner's future language development, tantamount to putting all the learner's linguistic eggs in an unsturdy basket. The issue for classroom teachers is certainly less one of the legitimacy of the goal of oral proficiency than it is of the oft-resulting neglect of the other modalities.

The conditions under which oral skills are utilized make them more susceptible to erosion or atrophy than skills in the other modalities. First, the use of speaking skills is geared to opportunity. Whereas listening, reading, and writing are individual activities in which one can be engaged at a time and place remote from the interlocutor; one rarely speaks in the absence of a listener. Deprivation of interactive contexts, due either to geographic location or motivation factors, will likely result in skills attrition, the rapidity and extent of which will be related to the initial fragility of the skills themselves. Second, in authentic interactive contexts where the focus is on the message, it is unlikely that a listener will provide persistent corrective feedback. Redundancy features of both the language and the context will help to provide for message transmission and lessen the possibilities for communicative breakdown. Thus inaccurate and imprecise speaker performance may be positively reinforced. Third, the nature of oral communication allows for a certain amount of avoidance and "cover-up" as natural ego-defense strategies. Having met the communicative needs of the desired level of interaction, further growth may be viewed as peripheral.

Educators have experimented with the use of other modalities to consolidate or stretch oral skills while providing a firmer foundation for future language development. Véguez (49), reporting on the oral perform-ance of students returning from the Middlebury junior year abroad, refers to them as deceptively fluent, clever in their strategies of avoidance, adept at communicating despite the language. His fear was that the overuse of these avoidance strategies would eventually result in stagnation and that these students would become merely expensively trained "street speak-ers" of the language. The solution devised was that of conscious *in situ* at-tention to these previously avoided language features through increased writing assignments while abroad: "writing at the college level involves the use of those constructions that the students were trying to avoid. It is more difficult to get away with not using them on paper (49, p. 10). Cortese (13, p. 8) refers to a similar problem characteristic of Intermediate-level learners who "cling to what they have acquired with-out trying to venture any further":

> Their active vocabulary is limited to that of stock situations presented in course materials, and their performance in any interaction outside these routines tends to be somewhat childlike—full of repetitions, set expressions and long winding paraphrases. For some people this "sur-vival language" is a mortal embrace: Locked within it, they eventually preface any exchange with an apology ("my English is very poor") never to reach beyond language-like behavior.

However, noting that those who struggle with the spoken word may be quite proficient in receptive skills, Cortese devised an experimental course in which reading activities paved the way for verbal interaction. The course revolved around a high-interest topic, selected by the students. In ensuing discussions students were encouraged to switch to their native language whenever they felt at a loss, and prompt reformulation in the tar-get language was done with the help of the class. Observing, however, that oral performance continued to consist primarily of brief utterances, Cortese concluded that a major upgrading in the quality of discourse was in order (13, p. 15):

> Training was needed in discourse planning, as well as in surface co-hesion devices; the students needed to become aware of where the problems lay, and this could be done more easily through writing.

Through writing activities and peer editing workshops, Cortese ob-served that students became more aware that problems of meaning de-rived only to a limited extent from lexical items or lack of grammatical ac-curacy. Thus, through developing the modalities of reading and writing and exploiting the nature of each of the skills, Cortese noticed definite im-provement in oral production as well (13, p. 22):

The variety of speech acts which the students could handle in connected discourse was substantially greater than at the beginning of the course. But it was the ability to convey point of view and illocutionary force, to match verbal behavior to its intended effect, and to use codes appropriate to the interacting partner . . . that was most rewarding, as one could see the participants actually doing things with words.

Such "skills chaining" procedures that exploit the central characteristics of each modality certainly merit further exploration. Byrnes (8) notes that the receptive skills, for example, are more stable, with reading subject to the least fluctuation even after formal instruction has long passed.

Skill development, however, takes time, and the time constraints of the typical foreign language classroom hardly bear restating. If one cannot change the external structure of the classroom learning situation, one must look for flexibility within that structure. Higgs (21) counsels that teachers and students should "do in the classroom only what cannot be done profitably anywhere else or in any other way," where "any other way" refers to the proper role of the instructor. The teacher who serves merely as a listen-and-repeat model or a lecturer of structure will be poorly utilized. "If, as foreign language instructors, our classroom activities consist largely of going over the exercises and content already found in the textbook, then we stand fairly accused of not doing our job" (21, p. 293).

The routinization of some of these mechanical, yet time-consuming, tasks might allow teachers better use of class time to devote more attention to individual learner needs and to serve in what must be the teacher's most important role: to create opportunities for interaction and for negotiation of meaning (Richards, 40).

Various types of grouping strategies may be helpful in maximizing students' opportunities for purposeful interactive language use. In a study on the effects of group size on student language-use opportunities, Nerenz and Knop (36) note that as activities became less teacher-oriented, the frequency of use of the target language declined, stabilizing at approximately 80 percent for oral activities. Yet, there was an equally striking increase in the communicative nature of the students' speech. The data indicated that large group activities, while characterized by more frequent use of the target language, focused more on repetition than on personal choice. Interestingly enough, even in individualized activities, students still used the target language at least two-thirds of the time. In terms of the most productive grouping arrangements, the study indicated that writing tasks were performed best on an individual basis, with pairs most desirable for speaking, and large groups or small groups (3–4) best suited to listening activities. While a very real fear in the use of grouping strategies is the loss of instructional control, the authors make several recommendations for the avoidance or reduction of off-task behavior (fooling around): priming with review or vocabulary; use of clearly defined tasks with specific outcomes and time limitations; teacher circulation; and demonstrable follow-up. Thus, the study offers one option for dealing with the familiar constraints of time and class size and indicates that peer grouping strategies may provide for more student in-depth use of the language, as well as afford students more accountability for their communicative efforts.

Functional Language Use

Over a decade of focus on communication in the classroom has produced a rich professional literature in the area of classroom teaching strategies. Nevertheless, producing proficient language users seems to involve more than the implementation of "role plays"; moreover, volumes of strategies will be of little use if they are not used thoughtfully. If teachers are not aware of the purpose and instructional fit of a given activity, they will have difficulty not only in adapting it but also in judging student performance through it, and in judging the overall success of the strategy itself.

Stevick (47) cites practice as one of the most important principles in skill acquisition; simply stated, we learn to do what we practice doing. If we want students to give and get directions, we must have them practice giving and getting directions; if we want students to persuade, we must have them practice persuading. The ability to hypothesize, for example, does not arise automatically from the ability to form sentences using the imperfect subjunctive; one cannot necessarily support opinions merely because one can link two clauses with the word *because.* The functions themselves must be developed, as Heilenman and Kaplan note (20, p. 63):

> It is tempting to ascribe the failure of students to successfully narrate and describe in the past, present, and future to inadequacy in the area of auxiliaries, endings, and vocabulary. At least a portion of the problem, however, may lie in the fact that competent narrating and describing is a skill that has to be developed in any language, including the first. In other words, learning how to describe, how to narrate, and how to support opinions is a cognitive skill as well as a language-specific one. For the oral skills in particular, this is a skill that is rarely the subject of conscious academic planning.

Joba (25) reports success with "function mapping" activities that allow students opportunities for task planning of a nonlinguistic nature. For example, prior to performing hypothesis-formation tasks, students practice moving from the abstract to the concrete plane for organization of thought by imagining themselves in the actual situation and devising questions, recording thoughts and observations. Rubin (43) has devised similar approaches to developing learner opinion-supporting skills: a problem-solving task is outlined, and students, in groups of five, simulate the roles of individuals with varying responsibilities for solving the problem. At the end of a given time period, individuals in the group rotate roles and must continue the problem-solving task from the perspective of a different character.

If the goal of language instruction is that of performing authentic communicative tasks, not only must students be provided opportunities to function in the language, but also classroom instruction must be examined for the extent to which (1) students are allowed to perceive the language as functional and (2) communication takes place within some relevant context.

It is crucial to any proficiency orientation that students see the language as purposeful—not merely as noise generated by choral repetition and somnambulent drilling, but as the vehicle through which meaning is conveyed. However, Higgs (21) has observed that the text explanation of a grammar point is not always indicative of its meaning and ultimate function in the language. While real communication is sustained with purpose, many texts, for all the wonderful cosmetics, remain oriented to grammar for its own sake. Were only one change allowable in traditional instruction in order to make it more proficiency-oriented, perhaps the change most likely to produce a profound impact on learners would be altering the approach to the concept of grammar. Present practices, which instill in students a system of labels and contrastive rules, literally demand that learners fight their way out of the forest of metalanguage and draw their own conclusions regarding the nature and breadth of the meanings and purposes these features can convey—conclusions which, at least at the early stages, will likely be drawn from their most available source, the first language. An example is subject pronouns in Spanish, whose text presentation commonly occurs in the beginning pages under the label "optional." The appropriate use of these pronouns, however, is not based on whim; rather, different meanings result from their inclusion or omission. American learners, told these are "optional," tend to link their meaning to the meanings conveyed by subject pronouns in English and therefore repeatedly include them in utterances where the meaning intended would require their omission. Not knowing that one of the meanings of the subject pronoun is that of emphasis or intensification, students will apply their own operations to express intensification, thus placing stress on the subject pronoun through intonation.

A second priority would be to allow students opportunities to acquire a rich and personalized vocabulary, one which, as Bragger notes (6) meets two basic criteria: it allows students to express real preferences and feelings; and it reflects current life-styles, interests, and concerns of the learner. Further, lexical items should be presented in such a way that semantic boundaries are known. The most obvious way to give students a sense of these semantic boundaries is to use the language as it is used in real life and to avoid random word lists and disconnected sentences. Bialystok (5, p. 110) notes that the context in which language occurs is crucial:

> Removing language from such a context, in effect, "decontext-ualizing" the language, has been assigned an important causal role in both the difficulty experienced by adults in learning a second language in an artificial environment . . . and the difficulty experienced by some children in acquiring literacy skills or in coping with schooling in general.

Slager (45) provides several guiding principles for the contextualization of classroom activity: (1) the situation should be relevant and immediately useful; (2) the content should reflect the level of sophistication of the student and his knowledge of the world; (3) the language should at all times be natural; (4) the sentences should have truth value—you do not gain anything when you ask the student to practice the same set of statements in the affirmative and the negative; (5) characters should be readily identifiable and their characteristics and abilities should be easy to remember; (6) there should be a variety of language samples through which the context is presented—the fact is that some structures occur more naturally and frequently in conversation whereas others occur in exposition, narration, and description; (7) the social dimension should always be kept in mind—that is, who is speaking to whom and the social status of each speaker—otherwise, there will be no possibility of learning the important distinctions between formal and informal speech; (8) in devising contexts, care should be given to alternate responses in real language use—if a student is asked to give a real answer to a question such as "where did you go last night?" he ought to have the option of answering that he didn't go anywhere; and (9) consider the "condition of elicitation"—should we ask students to make statements in order to practice their form or should we ask them to make statements in a context where a statement is naturally called for? How often, for example, in contexts other than classroom "reflexive pronoun practice," would individuals recite the detailed litany of their daily routine: "I get up; I brush my teeth; I comb my hair; etc."?

In terms of real-life performance, several other considerations present themselves for the proficiency-oriented classroom. Salient among these are (1) does the task reflect the nature of the skill area? (2) does the task reflect what the learner is able to bring to it? and (3) is the task "authentic"?

Reading activities should focus on reading. Listening activities should focus on listening. Since both involve the process of converting language into meaning, tasks which stop short of allowing students to assign meaning do not reflect the nature of the skill area. Reading aloud, for example, does not involve the comprehension process, nor does the familiar listen-

and-repeat exercise. The previous discussion of the factors underlying reading proficiency indicates that the process is not currently perceived as linear, but rather as multidimensional. Inherent in the guidelines are several continua which attempt to expose some of the phenomena readers call into play in bringing meaning to a text. Awareness and use of text features and organizational schemes greatly affect a reader's success: for example, the presence of subheadings and bold print; the author's use of examples and rephrasing; and the existence of connectors and direction finders, such as the *stop signals*—"in short," "in summary," "in conclusion," "finally," "therefore"; the *go signals*—"moreover," "furthermore," "also," "likewise"; the *turn signals*—"on the other hand," "nevertheless," "conversely," "however," "alternatively," etc. Further, Bernhardt (3) notes the reader's reliance on punctuation to capture meaning from a text. Such natural devices, employed by authors to communicate with a shared language readership, are often absent from prepared and contrived lower-level classroom reading materials. The latter are often dominated by a concern for sentence level syntax and morphology, with what the student has "already had" in class. Yet, by their simplicity, they may be depriving novice readers of precisely the kinds of clues these readers might rely on, forcing overdependence on their grasp of discrete linguistic features, and perhaps, as a result, ultimately fostering inefficient reading strategies.

The task should also consider what the learner brings to it in terms of knowledge and experience. The ACTFL proficiency progressions in the receptive skills reflect the predominant view of educators that both listening and reading are highly interactive processes to which individuals bring their own "schemata"—namely, their knowledge of the world, their experience, and their cultural framework. These background data drive the comprehension process, serving to set the parameters of a given message and establish reader expectations. Withing the range of possibilities that one's cultural and experiential framework allows, comprehension is produced through a process of validation which draws from both the linguistic code—the input of the written word itself—and the nonlinguistic clues as provided by context and supporting visual information. In reading or listening we do not proceed in linear fashion, stringing together letters or sounds to form words, then combining these words to form sentences, the sentences to form paragraphs, and then translating our final product into some message; rather, we seem to approach any act of comprehension with a prediction of meaning. Byrnes (8, p. 79) observes that the amount of nonlinguistic information the individual can bring to a given comprehension task is crucial:

> The less nonlinguistic information the user can bring to the task, the more difficult it will be for him to understand spoken or printed material. Yet, in an effort to arrive at some meaning at all he will

concentrate even harder on the linguistic signals, thereby creating a potentially serious bottleneck in memory.

From this view of the comprehension process, we can draw several implications for the classroom. First, comprehension tasks should be based on a framework of globally shared experiences. Bernhardt (4), in studies of reading comprehension, indicates that even in texts with lower levels of linguistic difficulty (most surface features are known and familiar), if the message remains outside the reader's experiential/cultural framework, misunderstanding is a likely result. Readers, in the search for meaning, will construct a model based on their own framework and subsequently validate their predictions by deriving significance from nonsalient information in the text. This problem becomes more acute when one realizes the extent to which reading in the foreign language classroom involves reading in the foreign culture whose norms, values, and behaviors are not part of the learner's experiential repertoire. Melendez and Pritchard (34), acknowledging this dilemma, suggest a series of pre-, mid-, and post-reading activities for sensitizing students to the cultural framework of the author. These activities require students to survey the text, form expectations, make predictions, and respond to questions which orient them to cultural factors in order to create a "mindset of readiness." Working in pairs, students perform further reflection and prediction activities at stipulated points during reading. Postreading activities require students to portray their understanding of the content through mapping procedures in which they *recode* the text based on its holistic meaning and develop some graphic representation, such as flow charts or diagrams, to demonstrate these deeper meanings.

Second, comprehension tasks should consider the reader's background knowledge of the topic. In a study of high school Spanish students' reading comprehension, Levine and Haus (31) indicate that topic knowledge could be more important than language level in comprehending a given text. Prior to reading a new article on a baseball event, second- and third-year Spanish students were divided into two groups, "limited" and "high," based on their knowledge of the topic as determined by a questionnaire. Reading comprehension was then assessed by means of both "textually explicit" questions, requiring direct recall of information, and "scriptally implicit" questions, requiring the reader to use both text and prior knowledge. Results of the study showed that the only significant difference on explicit comprehension measures was that of degree of background knowledge. No difference was found to be attributable to the level of language study. However, when implicit questions were used, the effect of background knowledge on performance was dramatically higher for Spanish 3 than for Spanish 2 students. Recognition of the power of high background knowledge on comprehension speaks to the need for several measures of reading comprehension, since such topic knowledge can bias measures of comprehension. However, it also indicates that the use of high-interest materials may serve as an excellent device for stretching learners' comprehension skills. In the classroom, the knowledge level with which readers approach texts can be better equalized through prereading techniques which provide relevant background data for the learners' use in approaching new information to be found in the text. Omaggio (37) suggests the use of visuals as advance organizers to structure readers' existing knowledge in preparation for the reading task.

A third consideration is that comprehension tasks should reflect the learner's developmental level. At the initial stages of developing comprehension, learners will likely require materials which do not force heavy reliance on an unstable linguistic repertoire, but rather provide for linguistic growth. Materials should thus afford a high level of predictability confidence, through reliable context and visual cues. Cummins (14, p. 125) suggests that the more context-embedded the initial L2 input, the more comprehensible it is likely to be, and the more successful in ultimately developing L2 skills in context-reduced situations:

> A major pedagogical principle for both L1 and L2 teaching is that language skills in context-reduced situations can be most successfully developed on the basis of initial instruction which maximizes the degree of context-embeddedness, i.e., the range of cues to meaning.

Although the guidelines in reading include in the early levels such materials as signs and advertisements, even these should be selected with caution—short or shortened does not always equal easy. Whereas the visual or environmental contexts supporting these texts may facilitate comprehension, the elliptical and semantically packed language may deter it. Because such texts attempt to convey much meaning in few words, many draw heavily from referents within a given culture. In other words, they strive for a direct route to the reader's mind and, in doing so, call up the readers' experiential associations. They may be, as Flower (16) notes, "saturated with sense," in that key words may represent a complex web of meanings. Teachers should select materials at the early stages that are neither context neutral nor merely context supported, but shared context-bound.

These same considerations take on perhaps more importance in listening comprehension, where the individual's performance may require more spontaneous activity. In order to capture the new information, listeners will require some familiar hook. The listening guidelines present a progression in which interactive contexts precede noninteractive contexts, the latter progressing to greater degrees of difficulty through, among other factors, increasingly greater information density. Interactional contexts would seem to provide more of the support features listeners would require at the lower levels of skill development. Such contexts, especially those providing for face-to-face contact, allow the listener access to visual information in the form of paralinguistic cues and further, under realistic conditions, afford the listener some degree of control over framing the message. Listeners in these contexts, for example, can request rephrasing, clarification, elaboration, repetition. This type of listening setting, however, is conspicuously absent, at least in power, in foreign language classrooms: while frequent interaction commonly takes place between teachers and students, as well as between students and students, testing situations at the lower levels are heavily geared to noninteractional settings. The combination of the features of a noninteractive setting, with scripted, tape-recorded speech, presented without visual effects or prelistening apparatus, containing new linguistic features as well as significant amounts of informational content, may produce an undue burden on the listener. Yet, such are the characteristics of many commonly used textbook-tape programs. While learners may be able to perform at higher levels in the receptive skills than in the productive skills, it may be precisely the myriad support systems, the clues, and the predictability that enable such learner performance.

Another crucial question is that of the task's authenticity. Does the task require students to read, write, listen, or speak for obvious teacher purposes or for authentic purposes—those for which the act would be performed in real life? We usually listen to a weather broadcast, for example, not to absorb all the details about frontal systems and high pressure areas across the country, but rather to decide what to wear the next day. In ordering items from a catalog, we do not normally read all of the information contained so that we can present detailed descriptions or answer questions about specific vocabulary. We compare and select items on the basis of how well the descriptions meet our previously determined criteria of size, color, durability, material, cost, etc. Authentic tasks are those which invite the learner to do what would be done, in much the way it would be done, by native users of the language. Authentic tasks have infinitely more appeal to the learner's sense of fairness, importance, and interest. As Canale (10) observes, it is this factor of "acceptability" that often cedes to more pressing practical concerns such as administration and scoring.

This feature of "naturalness" is perhaps most conspicuously absent in classroom testing where tasks, Canale contends, are often characterized by an intrusive nature—"the 'cold shower' imposed in place of more interesting and dynamic learning activities" (9). Concerns for authenticity should carry over to the testing situation where "classroom tests" might be examined for their correspondence with learners' "real-life tests"—the daily challenges they face in their (perhaps more important) lives outside the classroom. The latter "tests" are those that fall normally into place within the contexts of our lives and therefore have meaning and purpose; we know why they are there and usually what is expected of us in order to meet them. It is perhaps through this comparison that the artificiality of the classroom becomes most striking:

Classroom Testing   Real-Life Challenges

    meaningless, no context........meaningful context
    other-created ....often self-created
    powerless, no control............active agent, control
    expectations unknown ....expectations known
    impersonal.............................highly personal
    unwilling involvement..........willing involvement
    unimportant ....important
    little knowledge gained.........knowledge gained by self and others
    extrinsic................................intrinsic

Canale contends that lack of task authenticity may result in information of limited value: "To the extent that test performance does differ importantly and unpredictably from authentic performance, it is difficult to use a test score to draw firm conclusions about a test taker's true ability to use the language" (10, p. 352).

Certainly, what is done in the classroom can have tremendous impact both on learner performance and on learner views of the communication process; in other words, the classroom arena can provide students not only practice in using the language but also the skill of understanding how to use the language. Yet, instruction responds only to the "how" question of the teaching/learning process: how the language is presented, practiced, performed—the methods, the materials, the measurement. Instruction represents all manner of things done to implement a plan, to assist learners in achieving certain outcomes. In developing proficiency, two other questions thus merit equally careful consideration—the "what" (scope) and "when" (sequence) decisions of curriculum.

In terms of implications for curriculum design, the guidelines' focus on conducting authentic communicative functions prompts two important questions: What is functional curriculum? How would tasks be identified and sequenced for the various levels of language instruction?

Richards (40) describes such a program framework as one that is "organized around the particular kinds of communicative tasks the learners need to master and the skills and behaviors needed to accomplish them . . . to enable learners to develop the skills needed to use language for specific purposes." While in the best of all possible worlds, one would have access to such information regarding ultimate learner purposes, the generic foreign language classroom, composed of learners of diverse needs and educational and occupational aspirations, certainly does not represent the best world possible for language learning.

How, then, can such tasks be indentified? The now-familiar Threshold Level of the Council of Europe attempts to respond to this question through a taxonomy of speech acts whose performance would correspond to a certain communicative level. Yet, the scope of this undertaking stops short of more advanced language behavior. Students themselves may provide a partial answer to this question: In surveys of student-perceived communicative needs, for example (Harlow, et al.,19; Lacasa and Lacasa, 28), groups of university-level students of Spanish and French gave high ranking to the following: meeting people, greeting people, expressing pleasure and displeasure, expressing satisfaction, complaining, expressing want and intention, expressing approval and disapproval, expressing appreciation, suggesting, asking, seeking and giving permission, expressing possibility, offering to do something.

This information, though providing guidance, is not enough; it remains discrete and static and offers no foundation for further learner growth. In fact, limiting curricular planning at the lower levels of instruction to task inventories may actually increase learner dependence. These discrete purposes and notions bear no evident organizational scheme through which they can be transferred to the classroom and thus provide for the cohesiveness and transferability which seem necessary for learners to reach the level of independent operations. In short, there is no real sequential arrangement to be found in such information. The speech acts are specific-purpose oriented, and purpose bears no inherent hierarchy. As Valdman notes: "No principled basis exists for the ordering of speech acts relative to each other; there is no reason, for example, why promises should be taught before orders or approval before persuasion" (48, p. 35).

Whereas these discrete purposes lack progression, it does seem that the more global task categories, such as those found in the proficiency guidelines, can provide the curriculum developer with some sense of priority and direction. Since these ranges of function are tied to the amount and variety of interaction they would elicit, they can be helpful in establishing task realms for the learner. It seems feasible, for example, that fluent speech acts in the area of information gathering and provision would precede in nature and need those in the realm of conjecture and hypotheses formation.

But this information alone will be of limited use in providing a sequence of instruction. Decisions regarding course content and articulation require far more explicit information, specifically, regarding how these functions will be operationalized, since any one function may be realized through a variety of very different ways. To illustrate, one may select one of the above-listed tasks, such as "expressing want or intention" and, superimposing it on the various continua underlying the functional component of the proficiency progression, see that the particular function may be expressed at a variety of levels, each of which subsumes all the others. Expressing want, for example, at the transactional, declarative, and information-giving levels will require a somewhat less "sophisticated" configuration of formal operations than that required at the levels of negotiating, supporting, and hypothesizing. Furthermore, there is variety even within a given level. For example, at the transactional level, there are a number of acceptable ways, depending on the context, to achieve the purpose of expressing "want." In Spanish one might say, *"agua, por favor"*; *"un vaso de agua, por favor"*; *"quiero agua"*; *"quisiera un vaso de agua"*; *"¿me trae agua?"*; *"favor de traer agua"*; and so on.

In the preceding discussion of the criteria scheme of the proficiency guidelines, it was noted that the performance of a given function is bounded by the context and accuracy ranges of a given level, where accuracy was defined on a continuum in terms of such aspects as precision, cohesion, flexibility, and appropriateness to context. Criteria identify ranges not only in terms of how well a function is performed but also by what means it is performed—how the learner uses the meaning access system, or the grammar, of the language.

These considerations seem to indicate the need for learners to learn specifics of a given task performance and to understand how meaning is negotiated—that a given function may be fulfilled by a variety of linguistic means and, further, that a given structural element may contribute to a number of different functions and convey a number of diverse meanings.

Whereas functions can be identified in terms of learner-based criteria, context-based immediacy of need, or simply instructor intuition, and whereas the level or range of task performance might be construed by the global prioritizing scheme of the guidelines, these factors alone will not allow for the operational sequencing demanded for careful curriculum planning. If grammar is the means by which these functions are carried out, then grammar has an extremely important role to play in planning course content. Because we can identify the purposes and meanings conveyed by a series of structures and because a given structure can be combined with others in different constellations to fulfill various functions, the grammar of the language constitutes the underlying flexibility factor of language use. Further, while purpose-directed tasks may resist hierarchical arrangement, Valdman notes that "various pedagogical or systematic principles may be invoked in the ordering of structural features" (48, p. 38).

The mere mention of "grammar" is likely to evoke images of pages from a textbook: highlighted verb conjugation blocks; sections on *ser* vs. *estar, imparfait* vs. *passé composé, por* vs. *para,* or *connaître* vs. *savoir;* lectures on direct and indirect object pronoun use and placement; rule after rule and exception after exception. The word *grammar* evokes images of viewing the language from without, rather than using it from within. Grammar has thus come to be equated with rules, contrasts, hurdles, and mistakes. However, if one views grammar as "a system for converting meaning into language" (Higgs, 21) and likewise for converting language into meaning, then its role in communication and acquiring proficiency in communication cannot be overlooked. This view of grammar, which places meaning in a central position, the axis around which all else revolves, speaks not to the traditional grammar-oriented syllabus through which learners collect chunks of metalanguage, but rather to one based on a different set of criteria, which views grammar as a necessary means to an end—namely, the accurate and precise transmission and reception of meaning. Decisions regarding functions, based on available criteria, might be meshed with decisions regarding grammar, also based on available criteria. While no criteria for the latter are observable in the guidelines themselves, they can be construed through the manner in which the guidelines become activated through assessment. In other words, if grammar is the means by which functions are performed and meaning is conveyed, then one needs to take a closer look at the phenomenon of performance. While this section has focused on drawing implications from the content and notions of the guidelines, the following section will address curricular and instructional implications of the nature of performance, beginning with the grammar syllabus.

2. AN ASSESSMENT OF PROFICIENCY INDICATES THE HIGHEST OBSERVED LEVEL OF SUSTAINED PERFORMANCE OF AN INDIVIDUAL.

Assessments of proficiency, including the oral proficiency interview and the computer adaptive receptive skills tests under development, presuppose unique evaluative techniques, since they do not confine themselves to the examination of a particular set of behaviors but are open to examination of the entire universe of language use. Through a series of purposeful elicitation techniques, testers can challenge individuals into increasingly wider ranges of behavior. In assessing oral proficiency through a face-to-face interview, the real art of the procedure lies in the psychological plane, in the interviewer's ability to ease the candidate upward through the various levels, allowing full demonstration at each level, until the individual reaches the point at which his or her language is no longer sufficient to sustain task demands. The well-conducted interview does not proceed in linear fashion through a prepared course of interrogation. Rather, the process is most easily depicted by an ever-broadening spiral through which the interview passes, probing higher and/or receding in response to the candidate's performance; dipping back to topic areas exposed by the candidate to broaden them, branching from them, and exploring task performance through them. The process is one which alternates "consolidating and stretching" techniques (Heilenman and Kaplan, 20) to determine a performance "floor," and to establish a performance "ceiling." The assessment of an individual's proficiency range is represented by the highest level at which the individual can *sustain* performance—that is, consistently control the language to the extent described by the level criteria, with no patterns of receding from that level.

While individuals will commonly display "concept control" of the next higher level by peaking into it or "partial control" by longer periods of performance at the next higher level but failing to maintain it, neither one of these profiles would constitute sustained performance.

A well-conducted interview will accomplish its *evaluative* objective by clearly establishing this highest level of sustainable performance. It will also accomplish its *psychological* objective—to leave the candidate with a sense of reward and pride in performance, knowing that he has displayed what he can do. A poorly conducted interview may fail on one or both counts. In fact, failure to accomplish the first objective will likely lead to failure to accomplish the second. The primary sources of an unsuccessful interview lie in the manner in which the candidate is challenged or stretched and might be categorized as the following:

1. *Too high:* Stretching the candidate to a level far exceeding his or her competence can overwhelm, produce confusion, and result in the deterioration in performance of even that language which is otherwise familiar and quite routinized.

2. *Not high enough:* The interview which stops short of providing evidence for or against sustainable language use at a higher level imposes constraints on that which can be demonstrated and will result in an equally inaccurate estimate of candidate performance.

3. *Too fast:* Though efficient interviewing is much to be desired, an overriding concern for speed may result in lack of thoroughness and responsiveness to the candidate. An interview that becomes an interrogation—a direct line of questioning that ticks off grammar points —destroys the intent of the delicate spiral process to elicit authentic language task performance.

Implications for Curriculum

Interestingly enough, these features are also far-too-frequent conditions in curriculum planning and textbook design, and their effect is much the same as that of a poorly conducted interview: a frustrating and unrewarding experience for the learner. Translated to the area of curriculum development, they appear as the following:

1. *The too-high curriculum:* Much of present curriculum planning, based on the traditional textbook syllabus, represents an *overestimation* of learner need. While educators have been decrying the overambitious grammar scope of textbooks for decades, little seems to have changed. Underlying the cosmetic alterations which respond to a more "communicative" personalized orientation is the same tired and unquestioned grammar framework, consisting of equally weighted and uniformly drilled structural compartments. The durability of this scope is perhaps less a reflection of teacher resistance to change than paralysis in

the face of it. The feeling that "all this" is somehow demanded by those at "higher levels" produces the strong desire to cover as much in two to four years (or semesters) as possible. Such situations, however, are often the result of exclusive top-down planning which, having set somewhat arbitrary and often highly unrealistic goals for performance at advanced levels (if, indeed, goals exist), pushes language instruction downward and creates the familiar bunching and congestion at the early foundation levels. Bottom-up planning, however, which proceeds from basal level programs upward in articulated fashion can help alleviate this problem and allow for a curriculum that expands with the learner at a more realistic and profitable pace.

2. *The not-high-enough curriculum:* At the same time, much of curricular planning does not go far enough. Even the best of planning often reflects an *underestimation* of learner needs. Basal level programs, for example, which confine learners to sentence-level behavior and which save the "hardest for last" not only limit present level access to authentic use but also fail to provide for ease of future communicative growth.

3. *The too-fast curriculum:* The "too-fast" curriculum is one that lacks responsiveness to the learner by failing to provide a careful sequence for language development or by failing to plan for evolving language use. The linear nature of traditional materials which present a series of structural monoliths may in fact shove too much into the learner's fragile short-term memory.

As proficiency deals not with recognition or recitation of discrete grammar units, but with the ability to use them for purposeful, meaningful communication, so must a proficiency-oriented curriculum reflect this focus. Moreover, as the guidelines are activated in a purposeful and systematic way through proficiency assessment, so must instruction reflect this careful and cautious attention through planning. However, just as the proficiency interview does not resemble a traditional test, a curriculum need not resemble a traditional grammar syllabus. Proficiency-based decisions regarding grammar scope must be geared to reducing where there is overestimation, enriching where there is underestimation, and sequencing for use. Further, these decisions must be based on nonrandom criteria.

In proficiency assessment, performance is elicited with attention to three planes or dimensions: the *linguistic plane*—how accurately can the candidate perform authentic communicative tasks; the *evaluative plane*—what is the highest level at which this performance is sustained; and the *psychological plane*—does the candidate have a feeling of accomplishment and is the candidate aware of both what he can do and what he cannot do yet. It would seem that if proficiency is a goal of language instruction, complementary considerations would apply to selecting the learner's grammar for functional use. Thus, three concerns might be prominent: (1) on the linguistic plane, that learner performance be authentic and accurate; (2) on the evaluative plane, that each level of instruction provide for maximum proficiency attainment and prepare for future growth; and (3) on the psychological plane, that instructional planning provide learners with a sense of reward and the feeling that they are communicating. These considerations would thus prompt decisions based on real-life use as well as on pedagogical criteria.

The Linguistic Plane: Selecting Essential Structures. Considerations of authenticity reveal several criteria for selection of essential structures; among them are relative frequency of use, number of different functions or meanings to which a feature contributes, and degree of use across the four skills, as well as degree of transferability to different social contexts. Students will, at the early levels, require a certain amount of structural streamlining, for it is at these levels that strength, breadth, and relevance of vocabulary will probably contribute more to overall communicative ability than structural variety will. In planning for beginning instruction, a primary consideration would be that of allowing students to perform a wide variety of tasks in varying contexts without unnecessary linguistic baggage. Here, criteria for selection of structures might focus on allowing students to gain the utmost access to meaning from the simplest apparatus and prompt selection for early introduction of those structures with relatively high frequency of occurrence, as well as flexible and variable meaning-access potential in the language. Partial selection might therefore arise from the meshing and resulting overlap of a two-way analysis:

First, through factoring out the meanings of a given structural feature and prioritizing these as to both learner need and frequency of use:

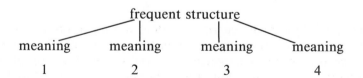

Second, through identification of needed or desired learner tasks with attention to the most frequent and least complex ways in which these tasks can be operationalized:

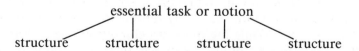

This procedure will help to establish the versatility factor of particular structural features and may prompt the deletion of those structures which contribute to the fewest high-priority tasks. Likewise, the process may screen for undue redundancy. Conveying futurity in Spanish, for example, a notion which would rank high in terms of immediacy of need, may be fulfilled by a number of different operations, with the most frequently used not including the future tense. Likewise, if several forms are sociolinguistically appropriate in conveying a given meaning or function and one has greater transferability across contexts, presenting all of them to the student at once could confound the learner with options precisely at the stage when communication is most deliberate and requires the most conscious decision making.

The various interrogative constructions in French, for example, are all presented in many current first-year programs in rapid progression, thus allowing students several options of varying degrees of difficulty for performing the function of asking questions. Yet, while students are likely to select the simplest option, or the most mechanical operation, the real target structure (i.e., the "right" one) for teachers is likely to be the most complex (Valdman, 48). Based on data indicating native-speaker perceived acceptability of these various forms, Valdman (48, p. 48) concludes that *est-ce que* deserves priority over "inversion" in courses designed to impart communicative ability:

> Inversion, which ranks in present practice as the primary target construction, is highly marked for formality and characterizes formal spoken style and the graphic medium. It would therefore be inappropriate to set it as a target feature in courses designed to impart communicative ability. Instead, that role should be assumed by the *est-ce que* which is at the same time sociolinguistically natural and structurally simple; for instance, it may be applied to any sentence and suffers no exception.

Reducing the "too-high" curriculum does not mean randomly paring down the amount of grammar but rather basing the selection of features on more performance-oriented criteria. Nor does reduction simply relate to considerations of amount but of what learners are expected to do with it. Expectations for full spontaneous productive use of massive structural chunks are likely to go unrealized. Further considerations in the selection of grammar, therefore, will also involve the unhooking of receptive and productive skills. In the previous example, Valdman (48) proposes a pedagogical progression for the introduction of the other interrogative constructions, one which more accurately reflects their distribution in authentic language use. While the more structurally simple and universal *est-ce que* is the mainstay for learner speech, *inversion* is infused through the written word and subsequently through speech reception, and in a later stage it becomes part of the learner's expected productive repertoire.

Thus, structures can be targeted for different degrees of mastery throughout the instructional sequence. Such considerations serve to provide for more authentic representation of a given structural feature since, as Valdman notes, some features figure more predominantly in formal or written communication. Further, they serve a useful pedagogical purpose, for the unhooking of these skills can provide for the consolidation and stretching necessary for global language development.

The Evaluative Plane: Planning for Growth. In addition to overestimating learner needs, much of present curriculum planning may stand fairly accused of *underestimating* learner needs by failing to acknowledge a well-accepted, experience-based, nonequation:

$$\text{taught} \neq \text{learned} \neq \text{used} \neq \text{internalized}$$

As was earlier noted, an assessment of proficiency at any stage will reveal user performance characterized by varying degrees of control over given structural features. While some will be fully controlled, others will be displayed with partial control and still others will be emerging and revealed only in terms of concept control. Though a number of different factors could be cited for the indirect relationship between what is taught and what is fully controlled, it can be concluded that accurate use of some structural features evolves more slowly than that of others and, consequently, that the later these "slower" features are introduced, the later full control or even partial control may be demonstrated. Curriculum planning therefore must focus not only on meeting immediate needs and consolidating on-level performance but also on laying the groundwork for future needs as well.

Beginning students display performance, for example, that moves gradually from word-level to sentence-level to paragraph-length discourse. If the goal is to develop discursive authenticity, perhaps to allow for its earlier emergence, then its features must be a consideration in curriculum planning, even at the basal levels of instruction. While a tacit assumption in current beginning-level textbooks appears to be that students cannot manage productive language use beyond the sentence level, data provided by Gadalla (17) on L2 learners seem to indicate that longer utterances and coordinate structures can be incorporated early in the sequence. Discourse strategies—such as conversation openers and closers, opinion prefacing, turn-taking, as well as constructions for deducing, concluding, and expressing causality—can allow for some concept control of discourse phenomena at the early levels. Moreover, learners should understand the contributory purpose of these features. Direct object pronouns, crucial to discourse coherence, are commonly presented in the first year of instruction in Spanish. However, Higgs notes the failure of textbooks to convey the sense that when these features are *not* used appropriately for shared information, "the speaker/writer seems to be metaphorically pounding the table" (23, p. 294). It is doubtful that practices which confine students to discrete, sentence-level drill with such features will ever give them a clear sense of appropriate use and communicative effect in authentic situations outside the book-and-pencil world of the classroom.

Proficiency-based criteria for selection of grammar would thus consider the full *range* of language use as provided in the guidelines and lay the groundwork for eventual performance at the higher ranges, beyond the mere reactive levels of transactional tasks. To illustrate through the speaking guidelines, sustaining performance within the Advanced range of the proficiency progression requires, among other things, performing the function of narration in past, present, and future time frames, with some ease, flexibility and cohesion and without disruptive error patterns. Such performance will require fully operating ability to convey the present, future, and past, as well as the display of coordination, connection, and sequential arrangement. Yet, in many languages, conveying the notion of the past is a complex feat. Spanish is a prime example: the distinctions in expressing the past are subtle and abstract; the meanings conveyed are without referent concepts in English; and the proper shifting of form to convey the appropriate meaning places tremendous processing demands on the learner. It is because of these demands that careful and early attention is warranted in curriculum planning. Research seems to indicate that it is precisely these more abstract forms that require the most exposure for internalization (Gadalla, 17). One might add that the amount of exposure is a significant consideration, and the type of exposure is as well, for it would seem unreasonable to expect students to display full performance control of such structures without having passed through prior *performance* stages of concept and partial control. Current materials, however, do not seem to reflect this consideration. A review of secondary basal textbooks, for example, will generally uncover "The Preterit" in all its glory and irregularity of form, as the last item on the agenda for the first year of instruction. In the second year, a quick review of the preterit leads to the first item on the new agenda: "The Imperfect." This is followed by the contrastive chapter, "Imperfect vs. Preterit," and from there attention gives way to the urgency of covering the other fifteen or so verb tenses. During subsequent years, learners repeat the study cycle, periodically reviewing the identical contrastive block.

Alleviating this repetitive (and, it would seem, less productive) cycle will require an accountability device which could safeguard against the randomness of presentation and use. A performance-based curriculum, directed toward student use of the language for communicative purposes, has the power to guide such efforts by establishing observable outcomes. Such curriculum planning can convert the vagabond teacher objective of "knowing the preterit" into the destination of using it for one of its purposes: the sequential enumeration of past activities and occurrences.

In much of current practice one might question whether ease of student learning is not sacrificed for ease of teacher presentation and, further, whether such a compromise is worth the consequences. The structural monoliths, the compressed contrastive grammar packages, the lack of distancing between complex concepts, and the nondiscriminating application of demands for full and immediate productive use certainly do not ease communicative growth; rather, they neglect it; indeed, they may retard it.

Kasper (26) observes that certain pedagogical practices may ultimately result in "pragmatic errors," discourse features which are neither used in a given context nor accepted as appropriate by native speakers. These errors may be *primary induced,* that is, arise from deviant input in the form of classroom discourse or inaccurate textbook rules, or *secondary induced,* the result of classroom practices or organization in course materials. The latter causes include inappropriately arranged exercises, inappropriately graded rules, and practice of some forms in proximity without previous explanation and practice of each.

The Psychological Plane: Fostering a Sense of Communicating. The side effects of poor sequencing, however, are far greater than this error induction potential. Lack of attention to course organization ignores the crucial psychological dimension—the need for learners to see their progress, to know they are communicating. As we noted, the art of the oral proficiency interview lies in the continuous attention to this plane through a spiraling elicitation process, which loops and expands, to ease candidates to their highest performance levels. This same art can be applied to instructional sequencing and allow for ease of performance growth through several "passes" at a given feature or a given function. In a looping and expanding fashion, aspects of a feature or more global function may be introduced for various uses and degrees of mastery and subsequently reintroduced for increasing depth and complexity in a gradual building process. Such a developmental approach will allow for aspects of the more complex features (those with higher processing demands) to be entered carefully and gradually into the learner's productive repertoire, while the simpler features may be entered more directly. It will also allow for instructional planning geared to the following types of decisions:

1. Which notions of a given feature are of highest priority?
2. Can aspects of a feature be introduced first as lexical items and later expanded and treated structurally?
3. Can some features remain at the lexical level as protocols?
4. Is this element used more in the written word than in the spoken word?
5. Can this element be presented first for recognition and later for production?
6. Can this feature be presented first for manipulation and later for communicative use?
7. Has sufficient "distancing" of complex concepts been achieved to allow for an internalization period?
8. Have redundant features (in meaning or form) been sufficiently distanced, contextually presented to avoid learner confusion?

The concept of proficiency, then, seems to indicate that we view curriculum not in terms of adding discrete components but rather as an unfolding, a gradual elaboration; that we conceive of language as a recursive process, "a development, that occurs through learning activities at all levels, which differ less in kind than in degree and complexity . . . that we conceive of language as having fullness, which deepens through time" (12, p. 30).

Implications for Instruction

As will be recalled from the earlier discussion of the guidelines criteria, the farther one moves along the continua, the lower becomes the predictability quotient and the higher become both the demands for self-investment and the need for linguistic flexibility. Yet, of all the decisions students must make as communicators, the one most basic is whether or not to communicate at all. Several conditions may tempt students into a mode of reticence: a topic that is not interesting or relevant, a task that challenges too little or too much, an encounter with the unfamiliar through unknown words or unexpressable thoughts. The resources required of an individual when performing spontaneously in a foreign language in the face of uncertain conversational directions are often not well-developed in language learners. Thus, the same concepts of consolidation and stretching implemented in curriculum planning and instructional sequencing must transfer into classroom opportunities for use of the language through the development of communication strategies and the encouragement of risk taking.

The risk-taking classroom stretches and challenges performance without overwhelming, through a climate of low anxiety and high motivation. Leontiev (30, p. 70) describes this ideal learning condition as "operational tension": "Operational tension is connected with the necessity of carrying out a particular activity: it allows a person to 'settle into' that activity and always leads to the best possible performance."

Thus, the risk-taking classroom will be the one that provides for task conduct through perceived learner needs, rather than through mere teacher dictates. Beebe (2, p. 62) suggests that in this regard, "communicative drills may be more effective than mechanical drills in part because the perceived gain or value attached to communicating one's own ideas may motivate more speaking and involve some risk taking."

The continua below plot risk ranges for classroom activity on the basis of learner self-investment:

No risk... ....Risk

Ego Involvement

pattern drill ....spontaneous interaction
conditioned response...............................creative response
lack of urgency ....desire to communicate
error avoidance ....guessing/trial & error
"modeled speech".....................................natural redundancy
predetermined meaning ....negotiated meaning
cultural isolation ....cultural awareness

To the left are represented the low-exposure activities, those demanding the barest degree of ego involvement. To the right are those factors which come to play in authentic language use where situations, topics, and tasks are unbounded by classroom constraints. Obviously, classroom activity that remains at the low-investment end of the continua will not provide the types of risk taking skills required for approaching and participating in real-life communicative experiences. However, classroom activity that, at the lower levels of instruction, forces students too rapidly into the high-investment ranges, is likely to create frustration, anxiety, and deterioration of language use and result in undesirable approximation strategies such as reliance on free forms or simplification of inflectional systems. In a review of literature on the topic, Beebe (2) concludes that risk taking varies according to the learner's social situation and setting. In terms of the former, learners appear to take greater risks when using the language with native speakers than when using the language with peers, "They figure that they cannot be expected to compete with native speakers, but they may be compared unfavorably to their peers" (p. 44). Further, individuals may take greater risks in group decisions than they do by themselves on the very same tasks (p. 43). Individual situational variables may also influence risk taking, such as the value of the reward and cost of failure, the degree of interest the participant has in the task, and the degree of skill vs. chance affecting the outcome. Beebe (2, p. 59) concludes that a balance must be maintained between the skill and chance factors: "We endorse moderate risk-taking as the optimal behavior, where students strive for success, keeping a limited reliance on chance and a realistic appraisal of their own skill."

It will be recalled that the interview as an assessment of oral proficiency is a spiraling process, steadily lifting the candidate, drawing back and lifting again to stretch the limits of the candidate's comfort level. This same looping process is applied to curriculum and course content sequencing, where presentation of new material is eased via the familiar in a gradual expansion process. Likewise, classroom activity, adopting this cyclical approach may serve gradually to stretch learners beyond the detachment range of language use—hooking into the settled, reliable, and familiar—to recombine and accommodate new information and increasing task complexity.

Larocque (29) provides an example of such a process applied to reading comprehension. By means of a two-dimensional grid, student tasks are gradually expanded, not only in reading but in listening and speaking as well. The grid contains a Reading Objectives dimension through which students proceed from scanning the text for basic information, to making inferences and perceiving text-related relationships, to personal involvement tasks which require them to relate information to their own experiences and invest some part of themselves in the activity. This latter type of activity forms an especially crucial link between students' own experiences and the classroom, as Larocque (29, p. 4) notes:

> This consideration is perhaps most obvious in students who are particularly unmotivated because they see no relationship between their own concerns and needs and the activity the teacher wants to do. This category of questions encourages them to perceive the activity in their own terms and to validate their own life experiences within their second language learning.

Through a Language Structure/Complexity Dimension, questioning techniques focus on expansion of both listening comprehension and oral communication, proceeding from short to open-ended responses. Though the process was designed for beginning foreign language readers, the use of prudent stretching techniques has applicability at any level; indeed, it may be the upper levels of instruction where *prudent* use is most sorely neglected.

Students will perhaps be more inclined to take the necessary risks of the proficiency-oriented classroom if they have a clear sense of instructor expectations and if they possess well-developed skills for coping with the unfamiliar and unpredictable. Confronted with linguistic tasks that lie outside the boundaries of a tried and true repertoire, learners will likely resort to the less desirable strategies of silence, topic avoidance, or shifting into their native language. Greater flexibility might be gained through the development of more positive and culturally appropriate communication strategies which help learners consolidate or pull together existing language skills for the performance of less familiar tasks. Such strategies may help learners focus less on what they do not have yet and more on what they do have, and what they can do with it.

In the area of reading, Hosenfeld, et al. (24) observe that, although individuals may have efficient first-language strategies, these skills do not necessarily transfer to foreign language reading tasks. Further, whereas readers' "plodding" foreign language reading techniques may not preclude successful comprehension, they do seem to influence the degree of efficiency and speed with which the task is performed. The authors recommend a series of steps to diagnose readers' individual strategies and to assist readers in identification, practice, and independent use of alternative, more appropriate, techniques.

In the area of speaking, circumlocution and paraphrasing are not always skills which are well developed in learners as they approach language study. Indirect discourse techniques ("he says that. . ."; "she thinks that. . .") may not only help learners develop skills in paraphrasing, concluding, and summarizing, but also provide useful and transferable discourse features. Fernandez (15) has students define English words orally or in writing in the foreign language by describing appearance, purpose, or location. Such techniques also call into play useful lexical reduction devices such as "thing," "whatchamacallit," "object," etc. Consolidation strategies can foster greater variance in expression, since learners will quite frequently rely on "familiar favorites," overusing the same devices and neglecting the others available to them. Joba (25) assigns students to select and prepare a brief in-class demonstration with one requirement: each statement of the demonstration must accomplish the function of explicit or implicit command in a different way: "do this. . ."; "then you should probably. . ."; "but it's necessary to. . ."; "however, I usually. . ."; "in other words, one doesn't. . ."; "for example, you can. . ."; "next, you have to. . ."; etc. Aside from requiring students to utilize the wealth of linguistic options available, such activities provide for practice in use of sequential connecting devices.

Investment of self in terms of content or topic will require simple escape valves for prefacing opinion, attributing opinion to someone else, expressing possibility or probability, and conveying indifference, as well as devices for leaning, stalling, and self-correction.

Learners' communicative efforts, however, are likely to be hindered without the interest, support, and gentle prodding of the classroom teacher. The proficiency guidelines, as well as the oral proficiency assessment techniques, bear important implications not only for learner performance but also for teacher performance. This is the topic of the following section.

3. THE GUIDELINES CONTAIN REFERENCES TO THE INTER-LOCUTOR.

The speaking guidelines, in defining assessable performance expectation parameters at the pre-Advanced levels, refer to the need for linguistically sympathetic listeners. Therefore, they assume the predominance of interlanguage behavior throughout the Novice and Intermediate levels. A sympathetic listener, however, is one who is accustomed to foreigner speech, not one who uses it. Yet, much of the language of the foreign language instructional setting is very "foreign"—representing a variety unique to classroom teachers.

One of the most difficult things to overcome in conducting an oral proficiency interview is precisely this "teacher talk": the nonproductive questioning, the impatience with silence, the corrective intervention, the evaluative commentary—all factors practically nonexistent in authentic interactive contexts. Since the objectives of the interview are to allow the candidate to demonstrate the furthest extent of his language use while keeping him at ease with his performance, such teacher behaviors, heavily reminiscent of the instructional setting, may prohibit the full demonstration of ability, as well as serve to confirm for the candidate, "yes, this is a test."

The interview procedure requires the tester to allow the candidate to produce new information, for it is only through the rich sampling of speech that an assessment can be conducted. Novice interviewers often find themselves in the "yes/no"–"either/or" trap, caught up in a questioning pattern which produces only a series of confirmations or denials from the candidate. Long and Sato (32) found the same condition to be prevalent in the classroom. In a study comparing ESL-teacher question types with those questions used in extraclassroom native-speaker/nonnative-speaker (NS-NNS) conversation, they found with ESL teachers a predominance of "display" questions (51 percent)—such as that typified by the following exchange:

> T: Are you a student?
> S: Yes, I am a student.
> T: Good.

However, this type of questioning was found to be virtually nonexistent in informal NS-NNS interaction (the target discourse for most ESL learners). Conversely, the authors found that referential (information-seeking) questions, which predominated in NS-NNS conversation outside the classroom composed only 14 percent of questions asked by ESL teachers in the classroom.

While such display questions may be used in authentic discourse as prefacing devices, to set the groundwork or establish direction for further exchange, they are used in the classroom primarily to preface complete sentence responses. Such elicitations, however useful during skill-getting or "focus-on-form" stages, are often unreliable in encouraging real communication. Kasper (26, p. 106) laments the fact that practices, such as complete sentence behavior, may serve to *induce* inappropriate communication patterns:

> In FL teaching, the pedagogic rationale behind this is often the practice of morphological rules which simply would not be applied if the

learner used—conversationally more appropriate—cohesive procedures. . . . It is characteristic of the traditional FL classroom that this
conflict between immediate pedagogic goals and the reality of communication outside the classroom is solved by giving priority to the
former.

It would seem that even in the manipulative practice stages, if learners are
to respond in "yes/no-complete sentence" fashion, the question should
have some semantic value and should provide the option for an emphatic
"yes" or an indifferent "no."
    Strangely enough, one of the most difficult aspects of conducting an oral
interview is listening to what the candidate says, not merely hearing how it
is said. Yet, in an interview, this content focus is crucial, for the messages
the candidate is conveying and has conveyed, regardless of linguistic
form, provide the topic basis from which the interview can branch. Failing to listen to what is being said results in senseless interrogation rather
than a tailored conversation. By the same token, in the classroom, when
opportunities are allowed for students to create messages, some attention
must be devoted to the message rather than merely to its linguistic packaging. Students receive vivid clues to where the instructor's attention is
being directed: the teacher response "very good" to the student utterance
"I hate math" is usually a clear indication that the meaning of the utterance has passed by unnoticed.
    Another clue students receive to their listener's focus comes from inter-
ruptive correction. In the oral interview, examiners must refrain from in-
terruption and allow for the flow of the candidate's messages. While correction certainly plays a crucial role in language development, it is most
profitably delivered and painlessly applied during nonspontaneous composition situations. In speaking, when students are struggling on the spot
to make everything come together, concentrating on the meaning they
wish to express and the means by which to express it, and attempting then
to deliver it in a fluent and comprehensible manner, correction is, quite
simply, rude. Intervention during these situations must arise legitimately
—because, as a sympathetic listener, one does not understand.
    Error tolerance, however, should not be confused with a casual attitude
toward accuracy. Omaggio (38, p. 50) cautions the following:

Until concrete and compelling evidence is provided that accuracy in
language production develops without correction of errors and attention to form in adult second-language acquisition, this writer will assume [that] careful error correction and concern for accuracy is important for the eventual development of proficiency beyond Level
2/2+. This means that the teacher who opts for full skill development
will need somehow to combine a concern for fostering "communication" with a concern for accuracy early in instruction.

The question, then, is not *whether* to correct but rather *when* to correct and *how* to correct. Immediate correction should more properly occur during those situations in which there is some degree of instructor control, during what Rivers (41) calls "skill-getting" and what Paulston (39) refers to as "manipulative" and "meaningful" cycles in instruction. Beebe (2, p. 61) adds that feedback should respond first to the area where the student perceives a risk. Frequently, students seem not to hear teacher corrections:

> Attention is focused on the uncertainty involved in communicating their meaning, not on the chance of making an error in syntax or pronunciation. They want a reaction to meaning, not an evaluation of form. . . . Teachers must respond to this perception of risk if they want students to attend to their feedback.

Delayed correction can occur after task performance and has the added advantage, as Bragger (6) observes, of addressing problem areas to the entire class rather than to one individual. Celce-Murcia (11) notes that correction strategies are more effective when selectively used, peer- or self-elicited, clear and precisely targeted, and presented in context. Rosengrant (42, p. 489) notes the potential of writing in this regard:

> The concept of "proficiency" implies an increased concern for accuracy, which can best be monitored through writing. What is needed, therefore, is a more conscious structuring of writing assignments so that students are indeed guided through a hierarchy of functions on their way to relative proficiency.

Another so-called teacher behavior which often exhibits itself in the interview process is that of impatience with silence, the reluctance to allow sufficient waiting time for response. In a study of postsolicitation classroom wait-time, Shrum (44) found that the mean length of time between teacher question and student response was 1.91 seconds which, she contends, "is only enough time to allow for sensory storage, a recognition and maybe short-term processing of very simple second language solicitations" (p. 310). Further, the duration of wait-time was significantly longer in the native language than in the target language. Based on this finding, Shrum (44, p. 311) concludes as follows:

> Given the frequent use of drills in second language classes, it is possible that students are answering very quickly but that the drill solicitations are simple and do not require extensive thought or attention to meaning.

Meredith (35) reports on success by forcing delayed response with foreign language learners, citing the view that impulsive responders frequently underuse their capabilities. In one study, an "imposed latency" treatment group was forced, by means of activated recorders, to wait 25 seconds before recording answers. It was found that both reflective and impulsive learners performed at a higher level of proficiency when a latency period was imposed on them than when they were allowed to respond as soon as they wished. In her chapter in this volume, Byrnes concludes: "For SL tasks we can assume that the increased processing demands present additional justification for longer waiting periods, particularly if thoughtful communication, and not just pattern-drill language, is the goal." Impatience with waiting may be a holdover from the rapid-fire drill era when constant off-guard activity was considered necessary, if only to keep students awake. Yet, in truth, teachers are probably far more uncomfortable with silence than are students.

One opportunity not granted to students in proficiency assessment is selection of the interlocutor. However, this opportunity *is* available in the classroom and should be exploited. It is not the instructor's responsibility merely to discharge questions, but rather it is to structure for creativity— to design tasks that offer the learner independence and provide for peer interaction. If the activity is not something only the teacher can do, often the students themselves should be doing it.

Conclusion: The Missing Link

The option of interlocutor selection is available in the classroom, and it is available in authentic communication situations within the target culture. Within these authentic situations, nonsanitized for the intrusion of cultural conflicts, all things can easily fall apart. Real communication is carried out between real people; therefore, among the decisions we must equip students to make as communicators, beyond what to say and how to say it, perhaps the most persistent and powerful is the question of "to whom." Indeed, to develop students' language skills and to neglect a sense of the cultural context in which the language is used may be simply to provide students with the illusion that they are communicating. Horwitz (23, p. 71) argues that "as with first language communicative competence, consideration of another person's perspective (empathy) is essential for second language communicative competence."

In its work on the development of the provisional proficiency guidelines in 1981–1982, ACTFL experimented with developing a parallel set of guidelines for culture. These guidelines used the linguistic criteria of function, content/context, and accuracy as their basis and attempted to define a progression of cultural proficiency in such a way as to facilitate assessment and instruction. As a result of this borrowing from the linguistic component scheme, the culture guidelines were somewhat artificially forced into an inappropriate mold, and they became confined to a series of learned behaviors, wedded to the content/context ranges of the language progression. The weaknesses in the resulting document are fairly evident. While the language guidelines reflect an assumption of a progression of increasingly complex linguistic and cognitive skills, the culture guidelines reflect no such hierarchical skills arrangement. Further, while intrinsic to the language proficiency guidelines are demands for spontaneity, flexibility, and the ability to handle the unpredictability of real-life language use, the culture guidelines do not reflect a complementary emphasis. Specifically, they fail to take account of two critical questions: how does a learner come to know and/or know about the target culture in addition to learning how to behave appropriately in it; and how does the individual process cultural phenomena on his own? Allen's comments (1, p. 149) echo the response of the profession to this experimental effort:

> Needed is a process which will lead the learner through a series of successive stages, culminating, perhaps, in awareness and knowledge of the culture, in understanding and appreciation of it, as well as ability to behave appropriately in it. . . . A new conception of cultural proficiency must replace [that] now in existence.

It is beyond the scope of this chapter to develop or propose an assessment progression for cultural proficiency; indeed, it is questionable whether such a progression can at present be formulated. This chapter has focused on many of the "realness" aspects of proficiency: (1) "real" from the standpoint of *observable,* that which an individual can demonstrate in the language; (2) "real" from the standpoint of *relevant,* the careful and correct attention to the needs and interests of learners; (3) "real" from the standpoint of *functional,* through a focus on language as it is used to perform certain communicative tasks with attention to the purposes for which grammar elements are ultimately used; (4) "real" from the standpoint of *authentic,* through task approach and performance, through discourse-length, contextualized materials, and through teacher roles and responsibilities. Yet, there is another, far more important, meaning of "real"—that is, *real* in the sense of "flesh and blood." Without attention to the culture to which the language is inextricably bound, discussions of proficiency, and especially of teaching for proficiency, will remain barren.

In all ways the concept of proficiency connotes purpose. This sense of purpose must prevail also in devising goals, implementing strategies, and linking the two for the presentation of culture. The concept of proficiency connotes movement and orientation toward future growth. Likewise, culture teaching must be directed not merely to rote memorization of facts or recording of anecdotes, but to developing in students the skills to confront, interpret, and understand new phenomena. Nurturing these skills may do more to prepare students to confront the challenges of later life and to appreciate the values and the complexities of a living culture.

References, From Defining to Developing Proficiency: A Look at the Decisions

1. Allen, Wendy. "Toward Cultural Proficiency," pp. 137–65 in Alice C. Omaggio, ed., *Proficiency, Curriculum, Articulation: The Ties That Bind.* Middlebury, VT: Northeast Conference on the Teaching of Foreign Language, 1985.
2. Beebe, Leslie M. "Risk Taking and the Language Learner," pp. 39–65 in Herbert W. Seliger and Michael H. Long, eds., *Classroom Oriented Research in Second Language Acquisition.* Rowley, MA: Newbury House Publishers, 1983.
3. Bernhardt, Elizabeth Buchter. "Cognitive Processes in L2: An Examination of Reading Behaviors," in James Lantolf and Angela Labarca, eds., *Delaware Symposium on Language Studies: Research on Second Language Acquisition in the Classroom Setting.* Norwood, NJ: Ablex, forthcoming.
4. _____. "Toward an Information Processing Perspective in Foreign Language Reading." *Modern Language Journal* 68 (1984):322–31.
5. Bialystok, Ellen. "Inferencing: Testing the 'Hypothesis-Testing' Hypothesis," pp. 104–23 in Herbert W. Seliger and Michael H. Long, eds., *Classroom Oriented Research in Second Language Acquisition.* Rowley, MA: Newbury House Publishers, 1983.
6. Bragger, Jeannette. "Materials Development for the Proficiency-Oriented Classroom," pp. 79–115 in Charles J. James, ed., *Foreign Language Proficiency in the Classroom and Beyond.* ACTFL Foreign Language Education Series. Lincolnwood, IL: National Textbook Co., 1985.
7. Byrnes, Heidi. "Grammar—Communicative Competence—Functions/ Notions: Implications for and from a Proficiency Orientation." *Die Unterrichtspraxis* 17 (1984):194–206.
8. _____. "Teaching toward Proficiency: The Receptive Skills," pp. 77–107 in Alice C. Omaggio, ed., *Proficiency, Curriculum, Articulation: The Ties That Bind.* Middlebury, VT: Northeast Conference on the Teaching of Foreign Languages, 1985.
9. Canale, Michael. "Language Assessment: The Method Is the Message," pp. 249–262 in Deborah Tannen and James E. Alatis, eds., *Languages and Linguistics: The Interdependence of Theory, Data, and Application.* Washington, D.C.: Georgetown University Press, 1986.
10. _____. "Considerations in the Testing of Reading and Listening Proficiency." *Foreign Language Annals* 17 (1984):349–57.
11. Celce-Murcia, Marianne. "Making Informed Decisions about the Role of Grammar." *Foreign Language Annals* 18 (1985):297–301.
12. The College Board. *Academic Preparation in English: Teaching for Transition from High School to College.* New York: College Entrance Examination Board, 1985.
13. Cortese, Giuseppina. "From Receptive to Productive in Post-Intermediate EFL Classes: A Pedagogical Experiment." *TESOL Quarterly* 19 (1985):7–23.
14. Cummins, Jim. "Language Proficiency and Academic Achievement," pp. 108–29 in John W. Oller, Jr., ed., *Issues in Language Testing Research.* Rowley, MA: Newbury House Publishers, 1983.

15. Fernandez, Yolanda. "Paraphrasing: One Step to Better Communication." *TESOL Newsletter* XIX (June 1985):58.
16. Flower, Linda. "Writer-Based Prose: A Cognitive Basis for Problems in Writing." *College English* 41 (1979):19–37.
17. Gadalla, Barbara J. "Language Acquisition Research and the Language Teacher." *Studies in Second Language Acquisition* 4 (1981):60–69.
18. Galloway, Vicki. "Perceptions of the Communicative Efforts of American Students of Spanish." *Modern Language Journal* 64 (1980):428–33.
19. Harlow, Linda L.; W. Flint Smith; and Alan Garfinkel. "Student-Perceived Communicative Needs: Infrastructure of the Functional/Notional Syllabus." *Foreign Language Annals* 13 (1980):11–22.
20. Heilenman, Laura K., and Isabelle M. Kaplan. "Proficiency in Practice: The Foreign Language Curriculum," pp. 55–78 in Charles J. James, ed., *Foreign Language Proficiency in the Classroom and Beyond.* The ACTFL Foreign Language Education Series. Lincolnwood, IL: National Textbook Co., 1985.
21. Higgs, Theodore V. "Teaching Grammar for Proficiency." *Foreign Language Annals* 18 (1985):289–96.
22. ———. "Language Teaching and the Quest for the Holy Grail," pp. 1–9 in Theodore V. Higgs, ed., *Teaching for Proficiency, the Organizing Principle.* The ACTFL Foreign Language Education Series. Lincolnwood, IL: National Textbook Co., 1984.
23. Horwitz, Elaine K. "The Relationship between Conceptual Level and Communicative Competence in French." *Studies in Second Language Acquisition* 5 (1982):65–81.
24. Hosenfeld, Carol; Vicki Arnold; Jeanne Kirchofer; Judith Laciura; and Lucia Wilson. "Second Language Reading: A Curricular Sequence for Teaching Reading Strategies." *Foreign Language Annals* 14 (1981):415–22.
25. Joba, Dorothy J. Personal communication, September, 1985.
26. Kasper, Gabriele. "Teaching-Induced Aspects of Interlanguage Discourse." *Studies in Second Language Acquisition* 4 (1982):99–113.
27. Kaya-Carton, Esin, and Aaron Carton. "Multidimensionality of Foreign Language Reading Proficiency: Preliminary Considerations in Assessment." *Foreign Language Annals,* forthcoming.
28. Lacasa, Judith N., and Jaime Lacasa. "Student-Perceived Communication Needs: Infrastructure of the Functional/Notional Syllabus—Spanish Point of View." *Foreign Language Annals* 16 (1983):179–86.
29. Laroque, Greg. "Using a Grid in Beginning Reading." *TESOL Newsletter XIX* (June 1985):1–5.
30. Leontiev, Alexsei A. *Psychology and the Language Learning Process.* New York: Pergamon Press, 1981.
31. Levine, Martin, and George Haus. "The Effect of Background Knowledge on the Reading Comprehension of Second Language Learners." *Foreign Language Annals* 18 (1985):391–97.
32. Long, Michael H., and Charlene J. Sato. "Classroom Foreigner Talk Discourse: Forms and Functions of Teachers' Questions," pp. 268–85 in Herbert W. Seliger and Michael H. Long, eds., *Classroom Oriented Research in Second Language Acquisition.* Rowley, MA: Newbury House Publishers, 1983.
33. Lowe, Pardee, Jr. "The ILR Proficiency Scale as a Synthesizing Research Principle: The View from the Mountain," pp. 9–53 in Charles J. James, ed., *Foreign Language Proficiency in the Classroom and Beyond.* The ACTFL Foreign Language Education Series. Lincolnwood, IL: National Textbook Co., 1985.
34. Melendez, E. Jane, and Robert H. Pritchard. "Applying Schema Theory to Foreign Language Reading." *Foreign Language Annals* 18 (1985):399–403.

35. Meredith, Alan R. "Improved Oral Test Scores Through Delayed Response." *Modern Language Journal* 62 (1978):321.
36. Nerenz, Anne G., and Constance K. Knop. "The Effect of Group Size on Students' Opportunity to Learn in the Second-Language Classroom," pp. 47–60 in Alan Garfinkel, ed., *ESL and the Foreign Language Teacher.* Report of Central States Conference on the Teaching of Foreign Languages. Lincolnwood, IL: National Textbook Co., 1982.
37. Omaggio, Alice C. "Pictures and Second Language Comprehension: Do They Help?" *Foreign Language Annals* 12 (1979):107–16.
38. _____. "The Proficiency-Oriented Classroom," pp. 43–84 in Theodore V. Higgs, ed., *Teaching for Proficiency, the Organizing Principle.* The ACTFL Foreign Language Education Series. Lincolnwood, IL: National Textbook Co. 1984.
39. Paulston, Christina Bratt. "Structural Pattern Drills: A Classification." *Foreign Language Annals* 3 (1970):187–93.
40. Richards, Jack C. "Planning for Proficiency." CATESOL Convention, San Diego, CA, April 19–21, 1985. Unpublished.
41. Rivers, Wilga M. *A Practical Guide to the Teaching of French.* New York: Oxford University Press, 1975.
42. Rosengrant, Sandra F. "A Hierarchy of Russian Writing Assignments." *Foreign Language Annals* 18 (1985):487–96.
43. Rubin, Donald R. "Project Descriptions." FIPSE Project Directors' Meeting, Columbia, MD, November 1984.
44. Shrum, Judith L. "Wait-Time and the Use of Target or Native Languages." *Foreign Language Annals* 18 (1985):305–13.
45. Slager, William R. "Creating Contexts for Language Practice," pp. 71–88 in Elizabeth Joiner and Patricia Westphal, eds., *Developing Communication Skills.* Rowley, MA: Newbury House Publishers, 1978.
46. Stevenson, Douglas K. "Beyond Faith and Face Validity: The Multitrait-Multimethod Matrix and the Convergent and Discriminant Validity of Oral Proficiency Tests," pp. 37–61 in Adrian S. Palmer, et al., eds., *The Construct Validation of Tests of Communicative Competence.* Washington, D.C.: TESOL, 1981.
47. Stevick, Earl W. "Curriculum Development at the Foreign Service Institute," pp. 85–112 in Theodore V. Higgs, ed., *Teaching for Proficiency, the Organizing Principle.* The ACTFL Foreign Language Education Series. Lincolnwood, IL: National Textbook Co., 1984.
48. Valdman, Albert. "Toward a Modified Structural Syllabus." *Studies in Second Language Acquisition* 5 (1982):34–51.
49. Véguez, Roberto. "The Oral Proficiency Interview and the Junior Year Abroad: Some Unexpected Results." Paper delivered at Northeast Conference on the Teaching of Foreign Languages, 1984.
50. Whitehead, Alfred North. *The Aims of Education.* New York: The Free Press, 1957.

3

ACTFL's Current Research in Proficiency Testing

Patricia Dandonoli
American Council on the
Teaching of Foreign Languages

Background

The following paper summarizes the background of and recent developments in ACTFL's efforts to develop proficiency tests in reading and listening. After a brief introduction to some of the issues in developing proficiency tests, this paper summarizes ACTFL's considerations in conceiving and implementing the tests.

As the emphasis on objective measurement over subjective evaluation increased in educational circles early in this century, tests that could meet statistical standards became the goal of test developers. The educational community, including the foreign language profession, put much energy into the development of tests that worked in the statistical, mathematical sense. Nevertheless, as several authors have pointed out (e.g., Ingram, 11; Spolsky, 19; Stevenson, 21), few tests grow out of the solid linguistic theory that should underlie them and which, in fact, statistical analyses assume *do* underlie them.

> The essential truth about nearly all kinds of tests is that the only theory they are based on is test construction theory, which is a kind of applied statistics. Current intelligence tests are not based on any coherent or explicit cognitive theory; language tests are not based on

Patricia Dandonoli (A. B., Clark University) has served as Development and Special Projects Consultant at ACTFL since 1982, where her responsibilities include fund-raising, corporate liaison, and project management. She has previously served as Special Assistant to the President of Queens College of the City University of New York and Research and Special Projects Administrator at Russell Sage Foundation in New York City. Her publications since joining ACTFL include "Survey of Foreign Language Enrollments in Public Secondary Schools: Fall, 1982" and "Recent Trends in Support by Private Foundations for Foreign Language Education," which appeared in *Foreign Language Annals*.

any coherent or explicit psycholinguistic theory. Their sole justification is that they work, i.e., one can make better decisions on the basis
of the information that they provide than one could make without
that information. [Ingram, 11, p. 7.]

Our understanding of language behavior and especially language learning is imperfect at best. The work of linguists and psycholinguists has shed
some light on the cognitive processes involved, but confusion within these
fields about the nature of language behavior, as well as the absence of cohesive psychological theories of cognition or learning, have precluded
widespread adoption of any comprehensive linguistic or psycholinguistic
theory by the language teaching and testing profession. A major impedi-
ment to the development of tests has been the lack of agreement on what it
is to know a language, what aspects of this knowledge should be tested,
and how these should be tested.

In the absence of an accepted theory of language behavior, can tests be
developed that go beyond a purely psychometric foundation? The practical answer is that they must. For all kinds of purposes, and for many audiences, evaluation of foreign language ability is a necessity. A major question, then, is how can tests be developed that make evaluation as
meaningful as possible without the fully articulated linguistic theory that
such tests require?

At a minimum, tests can reflect our imperfect [or "pre-theoretical," as
Ingram (11, p. 7) calls it] understanding of and hypotheses about language
behavior, as well as our instructional goals. The emphasis in recent years
on the development of functional language ability as the goal of many language programs has highlighted the need for tests that can measure the attainment of such proficiency.

Rossi (18) has prepared a selected, annotated guide to standardized foreign language proficiency tests available today. He summarizes thirteen
such instruments and rating scales currently available (several of which
test only English as a second language). Most of the tests listed date from
the early 1970s. With few exceptions, the tests represent norm-referenced
instruments that assess mastery of particular linguistic features or
subskills. Despite their inclusion in a listing of proficiency tests, most actually focus on achievement or attainment. Rossi's list reinforces the notion that most language tests in general use do not reflect the instructional
goal of integrated, contextual, functional language use but rather primarily assess knowledge of discrete linguistic features.

The Spectrum of Language Tests

Before discussing the specific tests under development at ACTFL at this
time, it may be useful to describe briefly the range of types of language

tests and how each is used, and to locate ACTFL's proficiency tests in this spectrum.

In the diverse and oftentimes contradictory literature on second language testing, several types of language tests can be distinguished: achievement, aptitude, attainment, diagnostic, communicative, and integrative tests, to cite a few. Perhaps the most useful characterization of the differences among types of language tests was presented by Alan Davies (8).

Davies developed a scheme that identified at least five types of tests: achievement, attainment, aptitude, diagnostic, and proficiency. He characterized these types of tests in terms of a time continuum, where X represents the point in time when the test is administered and Y represents some purpose to which the language would be put. His scheme is useful in understanding what is meant here by proficiency tests.

Achievement: ⟵———— X

Aptitude: (X)————▸X

Diagnostic: ———— X ————

Proficiency: ⟵— — — X ————▸Y

In this scheme, *achievement* tests (attainment tests are considered together with achievement tests) are concerned with measuring what has been learned of a particular course or program syllabus. Thus, achievement tests are represented with a solid line (known syllabus) and an arrow pointing backwards, indicating past time. Such tests are designed to sample appropriately from the syllabus content to enable the test interpreter to infer the student's mastery of the entire syllabus.

An *aptitude* test is used only predictively, to estimate, by using some measure of general language ability or ability in a specific language, what the test-taker's skill for future language is learning. Like the proficiency test, it looks forward, but only to predict future *language* skill. An aptitude test is built on the assumption that potential future language learning skill can and should be measured through first language knowledge. Davies' skepticism about this assumption is indicated by the parentheses around the X above.

Davies included *diagnostic* tests in his scheme despite the fact that he argued that diagnosis could be considered an aspect of the interpretation of several types of tests. He argues that in most instances achievement or proficiency tests so designed and constructed can be used for diagnostic purposes.

Proficiency tests, on the other hand, are concerned both with the past and the future, in that they not only draw on prior learning (but not a particular syllabus) but also aim to predict language skill for some communicative purpose. A proficiency test is concerned with the results of the learning process but not with how that learning is acquired. The emphasis in proficiency testing is on "the extent to which the individual is capable of utilizing his language knowledge of and facility in the language to accomplish some desired receptive or communicative purpose" (Clark, 7, p. 23). A proficiency test has as its content domain the operational definition of proficiency as defined by the test developer; scores are reported with reference to the examinee's standing in relation to the definition or scale of proficiency used to develop the test. In the chart above, the broken line to the left of the test, pointing backward in time, reflects the accumulation of knowledge by the student and indicates the lack of a specific syllabus.

Because proficiency tests are not meant to sample from a particular syllabus, they should not be used as indicators of classroom achievement. Thus, for most grading purposes, proficiency tests are inappropriate. Likewise, it is generally inappropriate to administer a proficiency test at frequent intervals; proficiency tests are more appropriately used at intervals in a language learner's education during which more significant progress will have been made. Proficiency tests may be used to fulfill entrance or graduation requirements, providing the requirements are stated appropriately and relate to the curriculum content instructional goals. They are also useful for employers who wish to know how well an applicant can use language in particular settings.

Not included in Davies' categorization, and arising out of the concept of communicative competence as a goal of language learning developed in the 1970s, is the type of testing referred to as *communicative testing*. Communicative tests most closely resemble Davies' proficiency tests in that they are used to measure a student's skills in using language in real-life contexts. Perhaps the most salient aspect of communicative tests that has been incorporated in some newer proficiency tests is the attempt to provide a context which is as authentic as possible to the test-taker. Many recent proficiency tests present tasks in both a linguistic and extralinguistic context, using language as naturally as possible. Thus, testing goes beyond the sentence level and is integrative and contextualized in nature.

The ACTFL reading and listening tests fit into the spectrum of language tests at the point where communicative and proficiency tests converge. They will be used to predict an individual's ability to use language for some communicative purpose and, to as great an extent as possible, they will be used ultimately to provide diagnostic information to teachers of the intended audience (postsecondary and adult language learners). The test items will not be drawn from a particular syllabus nor reflect isolated specific linguistic features. Rather, they will be based on the criterion measure of proficiency as described in the ACTFL Proficiency Guidelines. Ongoing research into the tests will not only improve their effectiveness but also provide empirical data for future refinements and revisions of the guidelines themselves.

ACTFL's Reading and Listening Tests Project _____

While it is not the purpose of this paper to recount the complete history of ACTFL's work in proficiency-oriented language teaching and testing [see Liskin-Gasparro (14) for a thorough treatment of these topics], it may be useful to place the ACTFL tests that will be described in this paper in a historical context and to acknowledge the contributions to their development.

When ACTFL began its proficiency projects in 1981, it had among its goals the development of a widely accepted metric for describing and measuring language ability. The potential benefits of such a system were compelling and reached into all facets of the language profession. For such a system to have immediate application, tests were needed that could measure the attainment of language proficiency using the metric as their foundation. Educational Testing Service (ETS) had begun work on applications of the Oral Proficiency Interview (OPI) several years before and had proposed a revision to the government skill level descriptions that became the precursor to the ACTFL Proficiency Guidelines. ETS's cooperation in ACTFL's work was pivotal. ACTFL recognized that tests in each modality were ultimately called for but focused initially on the Oral Proficiency Interview for widespread dissemination. There were several reasons for this, including the perceived need in the profession for a test of speaking ability (Brickell and Paul, 3). Primarily, however, the oral interview was selected for practical reasons: it had a long history of development and refinement within the federal government and was ready, with some modification, for almost immediate dissemination in the academic community.

In order to respond to the need for additional proficiency tests, especially in the receptive skills, ACTFL undertook a project to develop reading and listening proficiency tests. The project will ultimately produce model tests in Chinese, French, and English (with English serving as a generic model for later tests in other languages) for both listening and reading. For practical reasons, ACTFL has chosen to focus its work first on reading in French and English, with Chinese to be added to the reading battery. A parallel listening test will be developed later.

The following section describes the overall considerations in the design and development of the tests.

Considerations in the Design of ACTFL's Receptive Skills Proficiency Tests _____

Prior to undertaking this test development project, ACTFL organized a symposium on receptive language skills, bringing together experts from government and academia to address the special issues of teaching and testing the receptive skills. Several experts focused on the critical choices that must be made in designing a receptive skills test and made recommendations that could guide such test development in the future. The recommendations made by this group (Canale et al., 6) are presented below. After each recommendation follows a discussion of how the ACTFL reading and listening proficiency tests respond to the recommendation.

PURPOSE: Specific testing purposes, such as placement and certification, will no doubt vary from one interest group to another. Nevertheless, we recommend a focus on criterion-referenced proficiency testing that allows for compilation of both profile scores (e.g., separate scores for vocabulary and sociolinguistic sensitivity) and fine-grained diagnostic information (e.g., identifying strengths and weaknesses regarding particular vocabulary).

Criterion-referenced testing. Two main qualities of criterion-referenced tests have been summarized by Canale (4):
1. Criterion-referenced tests must represent, in a direct and theoretically sound manner, those tasks that are crucial to performance of the criterion task; while norm-referenced tests need only produce scores that show a high correlation with scores on the criterion task.
2. Scores on criterion-referenced tests are directly interpretable in terms of some actual criterion performance. Scores on norm-referenced tests are intended only to indicate how each test-taker stands in comparison to a larger group with little or no clear feedback as to the reasons.

If what we mean by proficiency is the ability to *use* language for some real-life purpose, then what we should want from a proficiency test is not only a score that tells us how well an individual examinee performed in relation to the others taking the test (i.e., a norm-referenced score), although such information is useful, but also a score that reflects an understanding of what the examinee can do with the language, in what situations, and with what facility. Such information is only available in criterion-referenced proficiency testing. By using the proficiency guidelines as the basis of the tests, direct inferences can be made about a test-taker's ability in relation to that criterion.

Diagnosis. For purposes of instruction, diagnostic information from a test is most useful. The capacity to collect some diagnostic information can be built into a computerized adaptive test through the inclusion of error analysis. While detailed analytic information will not be obtainable in the early stages of test development, it is hoped that ACTFL's tests will reveal rudimentary information concerning patterns of error.

ORGANIZATION: We suggest that the test be organized, when possible, according to two criteria: thematic unity, as opposed simply to coverage of particular structural points (e.g., vocabulary) or skill areas (e.g., listening comprehension); and the four stages of the Oral Proficiency Interview (OPI) of the Interagency Language Roundtable (ILR), namely, warm-up, level check, probe, and wind-down.

Thematic unity. Canale (4) has argued that test development should be guided by an "attempt to elicit the best performance from test-takers by presenting tasks that are fair, important in themselves, and interesting in themselves." He suggests that a test organized according to a broad theme (such as a day in the life of a student) provides a more satisfying and motivating experience for the test-taker. Thematic organization further provides a context for the linguistic tasks required of the test-taker, making those tasks more authentic and meaningful.

Thematic organization, however, poses the potential psychometric problem of item dependence (where correct response to an item requires a correct response to an earlier item), which must be avoided for accurate item calibration and interpretation of test results. Furthermore, a test constructed solely around one narrowly conceived theme would not adequately sample from the broad content domain of a proficiency test. Care should thus be taken to provide thematic organization within portions of a test while maintaining item independence and broad sampling from a suitably diverse content domain.

Another potential problem with a test organized around one theme is the possibility of interference of the examinee's prior knowledge or lack of knowledge. An examinee may have particular interest in or knowledge of a chosen theme that might account for uncharacteristically high performance on the test (a "hot house special" in OPI terminology—see Levine and Haus, 13). As in the OPI, care must be taken to be sure that the test adequately samples from several themes to avoid this problem.

Despite these potential problems, the advantages of an overall test theme or, particularly, of thematic sections within a test argue strongly in favor of their inclusion. Including several thematic sections or portions in the test can avoid the single-topic problem while providing the test-taker with some contextual information and orientation to the reading tasks to come.

One example of how this concept can be implemented is to have one portion of the reading test present the test-taker with a magazine table of contents. Some items of relatively low difficulty level could be devised concerning the table of contents itself. After successful completion of these items, the examinee could be asked to select a particular story of interest for further reading (and more difficult items). This type of connected context, while not fully embracing the concept of a thematic test, does go beyond an isolated passage approach and provides the reader with a more realistic task orientation.

OPI structure. The OPI is a "face-to-face test of foreign language speaking competence, lasting 10–30 minutes. . . . Through a conversational interview the tester(s) rates the candidate's ability to function in the target language on a scale of 0–5 [(ILR) or from Novice-Low to Superior (ACTFL/ETS)] according to a set of Proficiency Definitions" (Lowe, 15). The OPI offers the advantage of assessing in a reliable way a skill which has traditionally been difficult to measure. It further provides a face-valid measure of language ability that does not relate to mastery of specific linguistic features or to a particular curriculum but rather to a scale of functional language ability. Students can be assessed not only in relation to each other, as in traditional norm-referenced tests, but also in relation to an independent criterion as expressed in the guidelines.

Another important feature of the OPI in the context of this project is its adaptive nature. The experienced interviewer constantly tailors the questions to the examinee both in terms of difficulty level and content area. Adaptive test administration is discussed in more detail below.

To the extent that computerized administration permits, the reading and listening tests will reflect the four-phase structure of the OPI using the computer to mimic the actions of a trained interviewer/tester. The OPI is a "conversation" structured around the following phases, each with a psychological, linguistic, and evaluative purpose (Lowe, 15):

1. Warm-up: During the warm-up the examiner attempts, as much as possible in a testing situation, to put the candidate at ease. If necessary, this phase can serve to reacquaint the candidate with the language. During this time, the tester can obtain a preliminary indication of the level of the candidate's speaking and understanding ability.
2. Level check: This phase is used to determine the level at which the candidate functions most comfortably and consistently in the language. It serves to demonstrate what the candidate is capable of. During this phase the tester establishes a base line rating for the candidate.
3. Probes: Probes ask the candidate to attempt to function at a level beyond his or her tentatively established base level. This phase provides the examiner with an indication of the "ceiling" of the test-taker's ability, i.e., the level at which the candidate's language performance breaks down. The level check and probe phases are iterative processes. If the probes show that a candidate is able to perform at the probe level, the process of level check and probe recommences until the candidate's ceiling is found.
4. Wind-down: During this phase the examiner returns the difficulty of the test to the level at which the candidate sustained accurate performance, allowing the examinee to leave the testing situation with a positive sense of accomplishment. In nonadaptive tests an examinee often "works to failure" and leaves the testing situation feeling frustrated and dissatisfied.

Implementing this structure within a computerized format presents several interesting opportunities for experimentation. The parallel to the OPI warm-up phase in a computer-administered test can be used to establish an initial item difficulty level at which to begin the actual test administration. Several authors have discussed the problem of determining an "entry level" for an adaptive computer-administered test. This is all the more important since it has been shown that selecting an appropriate level of difficulty for the first item in a test can affect the overall test efficiency. Some have suggested selecting an item with difficulty at mid-point on the scale. Self-ratings can also be tried, since these have been shown in preliminary research to correlate well with actual proficiency scores. ACTFL will experiment with both approaches prior to final test dissemination. Whichever approach is ultimately found to be more efficient, each will be designed to accomplish the psychological, linguistic, and evaluative functions of the warm-up phase.

The parallel to the level checks and probes will take place as the computer program selects items from the item pool for administration to the examinee. Each item in the potential pool will have been previously calibrated, that is, its difficulty (and other characteristics) estimated through pilot test administrations. A correct answer to an item will cause the program to select a more difficult item for subsequent administration; an incorrect answer will lead to an easier item. Basically, the program will be designed to select items that provide the most information about the examinee's ability level, gradually coming closer and closer to his or her "true" ability. This process of item selection, evaluation, and subsequent selection in order to establish the proficiency of the test-taker closely parallels the operations involved in the level checks and probes of the OPI.

During the parallel to the wind-down, the examinee will be presented with several items slightly below the ability level established through the previous level-check and probe phases. This phase can serve the same psychological function as the OPI wind-down, that is, to leave the test-taker with a sense of accomplishment and satisfaction with his or her performance on the test.

TEXT/TASK SPECIFICATIONS: The item specifications should minimally reflect the interrelationship among four variables: performance level (e.g., on a 0–5 scale as used by the ILR), text type, reading/listening function, and reading/listening strategy. An illustration of such specifications is presented in Appendix A [included at the end of this chapter]. A variety of short-answer formats would be compatible with the reading/listening functions and strategies outlined in Appendix A.

The relationship between performance level and text type is complex. In establishing test specifications, it is difficult to avoid the circularity of describing proficiency in terms of what texts an individual can comprehend while at the same time describing a text's difficulty in terms of whether a person of given ability can comprehend it. It is important to separate these two variables in order to accurately measure the reader's or listener's ability.

The proficiency guidelines alone do not provide sufficient information with which to break this circle. Child (this volume) has proposed an independent typology for describing texts, but one that can be related to particular levels of the proficiency guidelines, as illustrated in Appendix A. These levels are Enumerative (Level 0/0+), Orientational (Level 1), Instructive (Level 2), Evaluative (Level 3), Projective (Level 4), and Special Purposes (Level 5). His descriptions are meant "to establish a scale graduated according to textual difficulty, which is in turn determined, at least in part, by the degree of shared information." This typology includes various aspects of texts, including the degree to which the texts are associated with or bound up with the external environment, the amount of shared information between reader and writer, and the linguistic complexity of the text. This typology forms the basis for selection of reading passages in the reading test.

One concern in the construction of the reading test is the possible effect of presenting the reading passages on the computer screen. At the upper proficiency levels, longer passages are necessary and may thus require several screens of text. This can be accomplished through scrolling or split-screen presentation, but the effects of these presentation strategies on the test-taker are not known. Later research will be necessary to determine what effect, if any, various types of computer presentation have on performance on the test.

Items or questions about each passage are constructed to reflect the functions or tasks associated with each proficiency level. (These are described in Appendix A under R/L Functions.) These functions essentially define what comprehension is at each proficiency level. For example, comprehension of an enumerative text *comprises* discerning discrete elements, since this is clearly the author's intent in constructing the text. Galloway (this volume) provides a discussion of comprehension in terms of how well the purpose of the reader in approaching the text corresponds with the purpose of the writer in preparing it.

It must also be recognized that in real-life contexts, readers are often presented with material that does not precisely match their level of proficiency. Individuals are often confronted with texts that are beyond their level of proficiency; yet they endeavor to construct some meaning from these texts. The revised reading proficiency guidelines reflect this phenomenon. For example, in the description of the Novice-High level in reading, the following appears: "At times, but not on a consistent basis, the reader may be able to derive meaning from lengthier material at a slightly higher level where context and/or extralinguistic background knowledge are supportive" (ACTFL, 1, p. 3). Items which reflect this lack of complete parallelism will also be included. For instance, an evaluative text can be presented and items concerning facts and literal information in the passage can be constructed. Too much discrepancy, however, is not realistic; in authentic tasks, it is unlikely that a reader would approach a highly abstract text in order to discern discrete elements (e.g., to recognize letters, words, etc.).

Item format. In order to limit the reading tasks to the test passages only, all items will be presented in English, although ACTFL may experiment with target language items at the upper levels. A variety of item formats is under consideration. In addition to traditional multiple-choice items, cloze and edit-cloze may be included. In experimenting with various formats, we are constrained by the requirement for dichotomous items (i.e., an item must be either correct or incorrect), the presentation strategies possible in the computer format, and the ability of a computer to analyze responses (such as free-response items). In addition to various item formats, several input devices (such as a mouse or light pen, in addition to a standard keyboard) are being considered. We are striving to require as little computer sophistication on the part of the test-taker as possible. Subsequent forms of the test may incorporate several such devices and approaches in order to experiment with what may provide the least interference to the test-taker.

ADMINISTRATION: An adaptive administration procedure is proposed in which the difficulty of items will be tailored to each examinee's performance level. Although requiring a bank of items to be available, such a procedure can, in principle, provide a more efficient, accurate, and affectively rewarding test administration than can traditional nonadaptive techniques. It can be delivered via three means: computer, trained test administrator(s), or multiple nonparallel test forms (i.e., where mean item difficulty varies from one test booklet to another and examinees select, or have selected for them, only certain booklets).

An adaptive test is one in which the items presented to the examinee are tailored to his or her estimated true ability level based on responses to previous items. In most *computerized* adaptive tests, the computer, at each stage of administration, uses the accumulated information obtained from previously administered items to estimate the examinee's true ability score. In this fashion the computer can make decisions about which test item should be administered next in order to maximize the total test information for the particular examinee. In an adaptive test, this process of estimation of ability and subsequent item administration continues until some arbitrarily predetermined criterion of measurement precision has been achieved (see discussion of level checks and probes above).

Several authors have noted significant advantages of computerized adaptive testing (CAT) over traditional testing techniques. Probably the most significant of these is the increased *efficiency* attained through the use of CAT. It is possible to eliminate from the potential item pool items that are either too easy or too difficult for each examinee. Thus, fewer items are needed to determine the ability of an examinee. This is particularly advantageous in tests designed to cover a wide range of ability levels (such as is proposed here). Some researchers have suggested that an adaptive test needs only half the number of items as the conventional test for equivalent results, while others have proposed that an adaptive test results in an 80 percent reduction in the number of items needed to ascertain ability. This reduction in the number of items is possible because only items designed to discriminate at the examinee's estimated ability level are presented.

While this theoretically possible reduction in the number of items needed to obtain an accurate score may in some ways be viewed as a distinct advantage, it also risks restricting the range of content of a test. This imposes a constraint on item writing to ensure that broad content sampling is achieved. Further, it suggests that some other factors be included in the test delivery system to take account of content sampling, as well as accurate ability estimation.

Other factors, such as the following, have been cited as advantages of CAT over traditional testing: there is no risk of test administration effects or clerical error; the characteristics of the answer sheet do not affect the test (although little research has been conducted on the possible effects of taking a test on a computer); test security can be improved, as can test scheduling; the computer is useful in test development (item banking and item calibration) as well as in administration and scoring. In an adaptive test, examinees are less likely to be frustrated or bored by a test that does not match their abilities well. Computer-based tests can be used by classroom teachers and others who may not be sophisticated in test construction; they also may be suitable in a variety of testing situations and for a variety of purposes.

Wainer's (26) often-cited extended metaphor of the hurdler can well illustrate the advantages of adaptive testing. In his example, we are interested in determining the ability level of the test-taker. In a hurdling test, this will relate to the height of the hurdles cleared. If the hurdles are presented in order of increasing height and a successful jump is represented by a 1 and a failed attempt by a 0, then the performance of a person could be characterized by the height between the highest hurdle cleared and the lowest one missed, with the following pattern representing a hurdler whose ability is approximately 55cm:

Height (cm):	10	20	30	40	50	60	70	80	90	100	110
Performance:	1	1	1	1	1	0	0	0	0	0	0

In order to answer the question of how accurate this estimate is, we might say that we were accurate to within 5cm (assuming the hurdler performed consistently with each attempt). If we wanted more accuracy, we would have to insert more hurdles between 50cm and 60cm. If we wanted accuracy to within 1cm for all hurdlers, we would need 110 hurdles. This would require a great increase in effort for most jumpers; and for those whose ability is between 50 and 60cm, the addition of many more hurdles between 10 and 20cm tells us next to nothing about the ability. For optimal accuracy and minimal effort on the part of jumpers, we would like our test to have the most hurdles in the area where greatest discrimination is required, that is, around the estimated ability level of the test-taker. This can be accomplished through adaptive testing.

CAT has become feasible largely due to the development of model-based test theory or item response theory (IRT) [see Hambleton and Swaminathan (10) for a complete treatment of the development and foundations of IRT]. Item response theory allows a researcher to compare individuals on the trait or ability in question, even though they may not have taken a test comprising the same items, such as is the case in adaptive or tailored testing.

In classical test theory, there are only two ways of comparing individuals' scores: administer the identical test to each or administer comparable forms of the same test to each. In IRT, comparisons are possible between two individuals who take different sets of items (i.e., different tests) through a theoretical link between the two tests. Through an underlying theory of physical weight, an individual being weighed in California can be compared to an individual being weighed in New York, even though different scales were used to take the measurement. Through IRT, the same type of comparison is possible with language tests (or any other type of psychological or educational trait or ability).

In classical test theory, a person's score is determined by the number of items answered correctly. Thus, using the hurdler analogy again, two persons with response patterns of 1111100000 and 0000011111 would both receive a score of 5. Further, it is impossible to differentiate between two individuals with scores of 4 and 5 and those with scores of 9 and 10. IRT, however, uses an estimation of the difficulty of the items answered correctly to produce an estimate of the test-taker's ability.

In traditional test theory, item difficulty is related to the proportion of individuals in a particular sample who got the item right. This presents the problem of relating item difficulty too closely to the group taking the test. Further, the difficulty of the item is not functionally related to the concept of ability. To estimate the probability of a correct response by a given test-taker to a particular item, IRT mathematically relates the test-taker's demonstrated ability and the inherent item difficulty. This allows us to escape from the tautology of defining ability in terms of those items answered correctly and defining difficulty in terms of the ability of the individuals who answered it correctly. IRT is a model-based measurement theory that makes strong assumptions about the relationship between a person's ability and item difficulty.

IRT has stimulated much discussion of the assumptions of classical test theory and of IRT itself. In constructing an IRT model, it is necessary to assume that an item or test measures only one ability, i.e., that the trait being investigated is unidimensional. While this assumption is also common to classical test theory, in model-based test theory or IRT this assumption plays an even stronger role and has caused considerable debate about the applicability of IRT to language testing.

Canale (5) has highlighted the potential dangers of applying a unidimensional model to what may be multidimensional traits. Other researchers have argued that the three-parameter model is quite robust and able to withstand moderate violations of its assumptions. There has been little research available to date, however, concerning what and how severe the effects may be of violating the assumptions of unidimensionality. Various approaches to determining dimensionality of a particular set of items have been proposed, with the most common being to factor-analyze the data. There is some question, however, about the applicability of traditional factor analytic techniques to IRT data.

IRT has an indispensable place in CAT. In an adaptive test, every individual is administered a (potentially) completely different set of items. Comparisons among individuals must rely on a strong theoretical link. "It measures the hurdles: assessing the empirical difficulty of each item. It adds up the performance: comparing the items correctly responded to with their difficulty and estimating ability. It provides a stopping point: estimating the accuracy of the ability determination and so deciding whether the test is over" (Wainer, 26, pp. 15–16). IRT further determines the nature of the test for each examinee, providing each one with items designed to most closely match estimated ability, thereby eliminating unnecessary frustration and boredom.

SCORING: Three general scoring criteria are suggested: accuracy of comprehension, independence in dealing with text (e.g., the examinee makes few requests for repetition or rephrasing of an utterance), and speed with which text/tasks are completed. These scoring criteria will no doubt be weighted differently and may be applied through machine scoring or by trained raters.

Items will be designed so that accuracy of comprehension is the primary factor in determining a correct answer. Since the level assigned to the text essentially determines the difficulty of the item, items will be constructed so that only one correct response is possible, reflecting accurate comprehension of the text. Other factors, such as independence and speed, will be incorporated into item presentation. For instance, at the upper levels in the proficiency guidelines, one distinguishing characteristic of the reader is the ability to read at what is considered normal speed. For items designed to test at this level, presentation of the passage may be speeded. Similarly, at the lower levels, the reader may have more need for aids such as glossaries and dictionaries. The examinee will be offered the option of using these aids through pull-down screens or windows. Thus, criteria such as independence and speed will not be used in scoring, per se, but these factors will be considered in constructing items designed to test particular levels of proficiency.

REPORTING: To assure that learners, teachers, and administrators each receive useful feedback, a variety of procedures is suggested for reporting test scores. These procedures could range from returning actual test answer booklets (with raters' comments) to each examinee and teacher, on the one hand, to providing administrators with verbal summaries of group performance (and norms, if desired) based on proficiency level descriptions such as those of the ILR or ACTFL/ETS, on the other hand.

Since these proficiency tests are not designed to be part of particular instructional programs and since only minimal diagnostic information can be provided at this stage, no detailed reporting is planned other than a global proficiency rating, sent to the examinee along with language-specific guidelines to describe the rating more fully. If the tests are later adapted for use in particular contexts, suitable statistics can accompany the report of the score.

CALIBRATION AND VALIDATION: Calibration of item difficulty should be addressed in three ways: by having receptive language proficiency experts match items with proficiency level descriptions (such as those developed by ILR or ACTFL/ETS); through pilot screening; and through experimental and ongoing use of items. Validation should be informed by a variety of studies, including the above calibration studies and specific construct, predictive, and concurrent validity studies. Content validity, as judged by experts in reading and listening proficiency, language teachers, and test users, would be particularly worthwhile to examine; such a study could serve item and test-editing purposes. Together, all of these studies would provide a reasonable response to the problem of interpreting test results.

Spolsky (19) has said that "the central problem of language testing, as of all testing, is validity." Validity, which refers to the inferences that may properly be drawn from test results, must be a primary consideration in test development and refinement. A thorough understanding of validity may require several investigations, and the process of investigating validity should continue throughout the life of a test, as the circumstances under which validity was originally determined can and often do change.

Four interrelated validities are most often used to summarize test interpretation: two criterion-related validities (predictive and concurrent), content validity, and construct validity. While these validities can be considered independently for discussion purposes, they are logically related. Rarely can a test be judged according to only one type of validity.

The following summaries of validity are taken primarily from the *Standards for Educational and Psychological Tests* (American Psychological Association, 2, pp. 25–30):

> *Criterion-related validities.* Criterion-related validities apply when one wishes to infer from a test score an individual's most probable standing on some other variable or criterion generally chosen because it is the best and most direct measure available of the phenomenon under question. Statements of *predictive* validity indicate the extent to which an individual's *future* level on the criterion can be predicted from knowledge of prior test performance; statements of *concurrent* validity indicate the extent to which the test may be used to estimate an individual's present standing on the criterion.

The selection of the criterion measure is especially important. A criterion should be selected that is itself reliable and valid. Often in educational or employment contexts, a criterion may be another test or a work sample judged acceptable in terms of content validity. In language proficiency testing, the criterion may be another previously validated and reliable test, or teacher- or self-ratings carefully structured in terms of content.

> *Construct validity.* Construct validity is implied when one evaluates a test in light of a specified construct. It is evaluated by investigating what explanatory concepts ("constructs") account for performance on a test.

> *Content validity.* Content validity is used when one wishes to estimate how an individual performs in the universe of situations the test is intended to represent. Construct validation is the process of investigating whether the selection of tasks one observes in a testing situation is representative of the universe of tasks (the performance domain) of which the test is assumed to be a sample. Content validation requires careful specification of the performance domain so that rules for item writing will assure appropriate representation of all facets of the definition.

It is important to emphasize that "validity is itself inferred, not measured. Validity coefficients may be presented . . . but validity for a particular aspect of test use is inferred from this collection of coefficients. It is, therefore, something that is *judged* as adequate, marginal, or unsatisfactory" (American Psychological Association, 2, p. 25). Thus, no test can be said to be "valid" without qualification: for measuring what, for what purpose, with what aim. Validity, then, must be interpreted in the context of the specific goals of and uses to which a test will be put.

Another point to keep in mind is that investigating the validity of test results is an ongoing process that may involve several studies. To be sure, some degree of validity must be established before the test can be put into use and is no longer considered experimental. Yet, ongoing research into the operation of a test is vital to keeping it current, complete, and useful. Indeed, the process of establishing the various levels of validity of a test can be an important tool in the development of a theory of language proficiency.

Further, no test is likely to be evaluated in terms of one type of validity alone. It is more likely that all three types of inference (criterion-related, content, and construct) will apply to varying degrees in all circumstances. For example, a test may be evaluated on how well it predicts future performance, how well the items sample the content domain, and how well it measures an explanatory concept. Guidelines exist which can help the test developer judge when to consider the various types of validity and how to set priorities for their investigation. In the beginning, a test developer may choose to focus on one type of inference, which may be sufficient to get the test into operation. Later uses for the test may call for additional research. Beyond this, for example, even if the predictive validity of a test is acceptable for its intended purposes, some investigation of its construct validity may make the test even more useful.

In order to establish an agenda for probing the validity of a particular language proficiency test, it is important to specify what is meant by "proficiency," as well as how the test results are likely to be interpreted. Upshur (25, p. 75) has pointed out that the literature on language proficiency indicates that it can be conceived as either "a relation between an individual and a situation requiring the use of language or as a psychological capacity of an individual which together with other capacities enables him to function in a situation requiring the use of language." For a variety of reasons, including test validation, this distinction is important.

In the former interpretation of language proficiency, which Upshur labels "pragmatic ascription" ("Someone is proficient"), there is no need to postulate the existence of explanatory constructs which underlie language proficiency. It is sufficient to delineate the behaviors (or performance domain) that constitute an operational definition of proficiency to the satisfaction of the test developer. Such a construal of proficiency and the resulting tests are useful for those who will make practical use of test results—those who need to make discriminations between individuals for purposes of placement, employment, etc. On the other hand, proficiency as "theoretical construct" ("Someone has proficiency") implies the existence of psychological phenomena which govern the behavior of a language user. While this construal of proficiency lends itself more readily to building a theory of language behavior, there is the danger that "the construct of proficiency has become virtually coextensive with human psychology. A test of proficiency becomes a test of everything about the individual, a test whose results are to be interpreted according to situational requirements by means of some incredibly complex computational weighting and combining model" (Upshur, 25, p. 83).

The "conceptual shift" from one interpretation of proficiency to the other is one which is made, as Upshur points out, rather casually in the literature, yet it is one which has significant implications for judging a test's validity. The type of validation one undertakes with proficiency tests will depend on which of the two characterizations one adopts. The former interpretation, that of pragmatic ascription, implies criterion-related validity; the latter, theoretical construct, construct validity.

While it is important to make explicit for the purpose of test development and validation which interpretation of proficiency one embraces, it is also possible to consider both to be important steps in the process of understanding and testing language proficiency. So-called pragmatic proficiency tests have great utility in the academic world—namely, for placement, articulation, entrance and graduation requirements, etc. Proficiency tests that meet these needs are undoubtedly necessary. But if test development is to be considered part of an overall research program, such as it is at ACTFL, a proficiency test must also be analyzed over time in terms of its construct validity.

If we limit our interpretation of test results to the context of pragmatic ascription, we can begin to focus on the criterion-related and content validities of the present proficiency tests. The test scores will possess content validity if it can be shown that the behaviors sampled in the test are a representative sample of the behaviors to be exhibited in the desired performance domain (American Psychological Association, 2, p. 28). This investigation requires that the performance domain be specified carefully. Further, "the definition should ordinarily specify the results of learning rather than the processes by which learning is either acquired or demonstrated. It should be sufficiently detailed and organized to show the degree to which component tasks make up the total domain."

Stevenson (21) maintains that the universe of content defining language proficiency cannot be sufficiently described, and as a result the demands of content validity cannot be fulfilled. We do not deny that it is not yet possible to specify with completeness all aspects of behavior constituting the domain "language proficiency." Yet we maintain that it is possible to use the proficiency guidelines as the framework for describing what constitutes the range of behaviors about which we wish to make inferences on the basis of test scores. Thus, while not perfect, the proficiency guidelines can be thought of as the content domain for language proficiency for purposes of initial test development and research. That is, they broadly delimit the range of behaviors, along with the context/content of these behaviors and their degree of appropriateness/accuracy, which completely describes the phenomenon being investigated. While this content domain may ultimately also reflect concepts in the literature on the nature and sequence of language acquisition (Byrnes, this volume), or may be underpinned by aspects of a theory of language behavior including various constructs, it is useful for pragmatic purposes as it stands, whether or not it does. It is only later, as the tests are studied for their construct validity and as we attempt to build a theory of language proficiency, that we become concerned with the guidelines in this regard.

In the present project, the investigation of concurrent validity and content validity will be undertaken prior to any thorough research into construct validity. To establish concurrent validity, test scores will be compared with scores of the same sample population on another, previously validated, test. At some later date, other criterion measures, such as teacher assessments or direct observation in real-life contexts, may be included in criterion-related validity studies. Special care must be taken in this adaptive format to ensure content validity for each test-taker, and exploration of the most appropriate approach for establishing content validity in this context will be continued. At a minimum, the item pool can be constructed to reflect the complete range of content specified in the proficiency guidelines.

During the ongoing research into these proficiency tests, ACTFL will seek to explore their usefulness in several aspects: as predictors of real-life language ability and success in language-related applications (such as jobs), as indicators of the range of behaviors considered to be representative of language proficiency, and as components in an overall research program aimed at developing a theory of language proficiency.

Conclusion

This paper has attempted to provide some background to the tests currently under development at ACTFL. This project has important implications for ACTFL and for the language testing and teaching communities. It is hoped that this project will represent one stage in an ongoing effort to develop, refine, and disseminate language tests that reflect the goals and priorities of the profession. ACTFL hopes to have the prototype French test ready for initial administration by fall 1986. At that time, pilot test sites will be selected for ongoing test evaluation. Later, the Chinese form will be completed. It is planned that following the completion of the reading tests, a parallel listening test (including interactive audio and video segments) can be developed.

It is hoped that the ACTFL tests will be used at selected colleges and universities for periodic proficiency evaluation of students, as part of teacher certification programs, and to assess applicants for various jobs requiring language proficiency. ACTFL will devise a system for dissemination and administration that will ensure the ongoing maintenance of the tests.

APPENDIX A. Text and Task Specifications for Reading (R) and Listening (L)

Level	Text Type	R/L Function	R/L Strategy
0/0+	Enumerative (numbers, names, street signs, isolated words/phrases)	Discern discrete elements	Recognize memorized elements
1	Orientational (simplest connected text, such as concrete descriptions)	Identify main idea	Skim, scan
2	Instructive (simple authentic text in familiar contexts and in predictable sequence)	Understand facts, literal information	Decode, classify
3	Evaluative (authentic text on unfamiliar topics)	Grasp ideas and implications	Infer, guess, hypothesize, interpret
4	Projective (all styles and forms of text for professional needs or for general public)	Deal with unpredictability and cultural references	Analyze, verify, extend hypotheses
5	Special purposes (extremely difficult and abstract text)	Equivalent to educated native reader/listener	All those used by educated native reader/listener

From: Canale, et al. (6, p. 391)

Notes

ACTFL gratefully acknowledges the contributions of several individuals who participated in the early planning discussions for these tests and who have continued to provide valuable input to the project. In 1982, Dr. June K. Phillips (later to become Consultant Director to this ACTFL test development project), Dr. Alice

Omaggio, and Dr. Charles Hancock (then ACTFL President) conferred with ACTFL staff on the proposed design of new reading tests. After these early meetings, individuals from the project's funding agency participated in further planning and conceptualization. Two individuals, Drs. Esin Kaya-Carton and Aaron Carton, have been selected to direct the project for ACTFL. A group of test consultants, including Michael Canale, David V. Hiple, Judith E. Liskin-Gasparro, and Galal Walker, agreed to advise ACTFL on test design and construction. Several others have contributed their time and expertise to this project and, though they are too numerous to acknowledge individually, their input has been tremendously valuable to what is a very exciting and ambitious undertaking.

References, ACTFL's Current Research in Proficiency Testing

1. *ACTFL Proficiency Guidelines.* Hastings-on-Hudson, NY: American Council on the Teaching of Foreign Languages, 1985.
2. American Psychological Association. *Standards for Educational and Psychological Tests.* Washington, D.C.: American Psychological Association, 1975.
3. Brickell, Henry M., and Regina H. Paul. "Ready for the 80's?: A Look at Foreign Language Teachers and Teaching at the Start of the Decade." *Foreign Language Annals* 3 (1982):169–87.
4. Canale, Michael. "Considerations in the Testing of Reading and Listening Proficiency." *Foreign Language Annals* 4 (1984):349–57.
5. _____. "The Promise and Threat of Computerized Adaptive Assessment of Reading Comprehension," in Charles Stansfield, ed., *Technology in Language Testing.* Washington, D.C.: Teachers of English to Speakers of Other Languages, forthcoming.
6. _____,et al. "The Testing of Reading and Listening Proficiency: A Synthesis." *Foreign Language Annals* 4 (1984):389–92.
7. Clark, John L. D. "Psychometric Considerations in Language Testing," pp. 15–30 in Bernard Spolsky, ed., *Approaches to Language Testing.* Advances in Language Testing Series, vol. 2. Arlington, VA: Center for Applied Linguistics, 1978.
8. Davies, Alan. "Introduction," pp. 1–18 in Alan Davies, ed., *Language Testing Symposium: A Psycholinguistic Approach.* London: Oxford University Press, 1968.
9. Green, Bert F. "Adaptive Testing by Computer," pp. 5–12 in R. B. Edstrom, ed., *Measurement, Technology and Individuality in Education.* New Directions in Testing and Measurement Series, vol. 17. San Francisco: Josey-Bass, 1983.
10. Hambleton, Ronald K., and Hariharan Swaminathan. *Item Response Theory: Principles and Applications.* Evaluation in Education and Human Services Series. Boston: Kluwer-Nijhoff Publishing, 1985.
11. Ingram, Elisabeth. "The Psycholinguistic Basis," pp. 1–14 in Bernard Spolsky, ed., *Approaches to Language Testing.* Advances in Language Testing Series, vol. 2. Arlington, VA: Center for Applied Linguistics, 1978.
12. Kreitzberg, Charles B., et al. "Computerized Adaptive Testing: Principles and Directions." *Computers and Education* 2 (1978):319–29.
13. Levine, Martin G., and George G. Haus. "The Effect of Background Knowledge on the Reading Comprehension of Second Language Learners." *Foreign Language Annals* 5 (1985):391–97.
14. Liskin-Gasparro, Judith E. "The ACTFL Proficiency Guidelines: A Historical Perspective," pp. 11–42 in Theodore V. Higgs, ed., *Teaching for Proficiency, the Organizing Principle.* The ACTFL Foreign Language Education Series. Lincolnwood, IL: National Textbook Company, 1984.

15. Lowe, Pardee, Jr. *Handbook on Question Types and Their Use in LS Oral Proficiency Tests.* Washington, D.C.: CIA Language School, 1980.

16. _____. *Manual for LS Oral Interview Workshops.* Washington, D.C.: CIA Language School, mimeo.

17. Peterson, Calvin R., and Francis A. Cartier. "Some Theoretical Problems and Practical Solutions in Proficiency Test Validation," pp. 105–18 in Randall L. Jones and Bernard Spolsky, eds., *Testing Language Proficiency.* Arlington, VA: Center for Applied Linguistics, 1975.

18. Rossi, Gary J. "A Selected, Annotated Guide to Language Proficiency Tests." *The French Review* 6 (1983):840–58.

19. Spolsky, Bernard. "Language Testing: The Problem of Validation." *TESOL Quarterly* 2 (1968):82–94.

20. _____. "Introduction: Linguistics and Language Tester," pp. v–x in Bernard Spolsky, ed., *Approaches to Language Testing.* Advances in Language Testing Series. Arlington, VA: Center for Applied Linguistics, 1978.

21. Stevenson, Douglas K. "Beyond Faith and Face Validity: The Multitrait-Multimethod Matrix and the Convergent and Discriminant Validity of Oral Proficiency Tests," pp. 37–61 in Adrian S. Palmer et al., eds., *The Construct Validation of Tests of Communicative Competence.* Washington, D.C.: Teachers of English to Speakers of Other Languages, 1981.

22. Stocking, M. L., and F. M. Lord. "Developing a Common Metric in Item Response Theory." *Applied Psychological Measurement* 7 (1983):201–10.

23. Traub, R. E., and R. G. Wolfe, "Latent Trait Theories and the Assessment of Educational Achievement," pp. 377–435 in D. C. Berliner, ed., *Review of Research in Education.* Washington, D.C.: American Educational Research Association, 1981.

24. Tung, Peter. "Evaluating Computerized Adaptive Testing: A Psychometric Perspective," mimeo, 1983.

25. Upshur, John A. "Functional Proficiency Theory and a Research Role for Language Tests," pp. 75–100 in Eugene J. Brière and Frances Butler Hinofotis, eds., *Concepts in Language Testing: Some Recent Studies.* Washington, D.C.: Teachers of English to Speakers of Other Languages, 1979.

26. Wainer, Howard. "On Item Response Theory and Computerized Adaptive Tests." *The Journal of College Admissions* 4 (1983):9–16.

4

Language Proficiency Levels
and the Typology of Texts

James R. Child
Interagency Language Roundtable
Testing Committee

Introduction

For many years the government community concerned with the teaching, testing, and use of foreign language has relied heavily on the excellent behavioral definitions of four language skills and five skill levels originally developed by the Foreign Service Institute (FSI) of the Department of State and, particularly in recent years, refined by representatives from several agencies on the Interagency Language Roundtable (ILR). The community has, however, lacked a textually based set of descriptions that would provide a frame of reference for the elements of language produced or comprehended at the five levels. In this paper I have attempted to develop such a system, which, if successful, will provide standards for language curricula and testing of value to teachers and resource managers.

James R. Child (A.B., Princeton University; M.A., University of Pennsylvania) holds degrees in German Language and Literature and Baltic and Slavic Philology. From 1951 to the present, he has served in various linguistic capacities in the Department of Defense, among them as language teacher and designer of language proficiency tests. In 1974 he and Emery Tetrault coauthored "Contextual Testing" which appeared in *Testing Language Proficiency,* and in 1984 his article "Testing Language Proficiency in the Receptive Skills: Native vs. Learner Performance" was published in *Foreign Language Annals.* For the last several years he has served on the Interagency Language Roundtable Testing Committee.

Author's note: I read the original version of this paper at the pre-Georgetown University Round Table in March 1981. At that time there were plans to include it, along with a number of other papers, in a pre-GURT collection. In view of that, I rewrote it with generous editorial assistance from Dr. James Frith, former dean of the Language School of the Foreign Service Institute, and had it ready for publication in April 1982, but for reasons too complex to go into here, the projected volume did not materialize. (Nevertheless, the 1982 version of the paper has been widely and informally distributed.) I have now revised it a third time, making several minor changes, as well as adding a section on the approaches raters may take to evaluate performance on the Oral Interview test.

97

My approach to this complicated issue is based on analyzing connected discourse, spoken and written (in other words, texts) produced by native speakers of a particular language (English). In collaboration with several colleagues, I have tentatively identified four textual levels based on a sizable number and wide variety of written (or taped) texts in the formal varieties of written and spoken English. The descriptions of these levels must, of course, cover not only the originally selected materials but also all others (including future texts); to date they have proved powerful enough to do this when applied not only to English but also to a wide variety of other languages. I must stress that our system has not been refined to the point that it can be instantly applied to the five levels of language behavior identified by the ILR. The government community is making excellent progress, however, toward this end despite the different points of departure of the two schemes. Before considering textual classification in detail, I will comment briefly on the ILR statements to which government linguists have, in general, subscribed over three decades.

Skill Levels

The original FSI descriptions were certainly motivated by the needs of language learning and teaching rather than by an interest in the more abstract aspects of textual analysis. Faced with the requirement to teach foreign languages to students whose main concerns were not academic but rather official and social, language teachers and testers reviewed a wide range of language situations in which the students would find themselves one day. They then grouped these in an ascending scale of situational complexity which has implications for the teaching and testing of linguistic structures. A five-tier system resulted that described the kinds of language behaviors associated with different social and professional activities and that established norms for persons to be engaged in those activities. The system covers an enormous range of communicative competence and performance, such as the following: "Able to read some personal and place names . . . " (Reading, Level 1) to "Can read extremely difficult and complex prose . . . " (Reading, Level 5). The descriptions of the four language skills and the desired levels of achievement have been continually refined within the ILR to make them more sensitive to the communicative requirements of language transactions at all levels, encompassing as wide a variety of foreseeable situations as possible. [These efforts have now been joined by language researchers and teachers who have designed a basically parallel system for the academic community under the aegis of the American Council on the Teaching of Foreign Languages (ACTFL) and the Educational Testing Service (ETS).]

Assessment of Skill Level

The measure most frequently used to determine the skill level of language learners has been the Oral Interview (OI) test. I will not discuss the OI at any length here since the basic purpose of this paper is to attempt to classify textual types from texts already realized by native speakers/writers rather than the "emerging" texts which are necessarily the product of an exchange between a second language learner and an evaluator of his or her performance.

Nonetheless, the OI does give rise to some interesting issues, because it obviously entails some kind of rating procedure. If, for example, learners are to be tested against textual criteria which require them to develop a plot, argument, or other narrative form, their ability to produce a coherent (semantic) whole will be emphasized. On the other hand, if they are basically to be evaluated for their knowledge of inflexional forms and their distribution (i.e., syntactic knowledge), they will be rated on formal, as opposed to communicative, competence. The difference between the formal and communicative approaches can spell trouble for interrater (and interorganizational) reliability, because raters using the former approach sometimes focus on discrete points to the detriment of overall communication. However, it should be noted that the wording of both the ILR and the ACTFL skill level statements generally accords first place to communicative activity (i.e., the need to transmit and receive message content), with restricted space given to formal considerations. This relatively new emphasis strongly suggests that textual criteria should be used to the extent possible by raters in reaching their decisions. With this in mind, I shall discuss problems surrounding texts and textual analysis.

Texts

As I noted earlier, the word *text* refers to any kind of connected discourse, written or spoken; it does not subsume other systems of communication, such as sign language, gestures, semaphores, and the like. For the present purpose I will consider texts against the backdrop of language levels and classify them from the simplest to the most complex, principally according to the communicative intent of the participants who originate them and respond to them, and secondarily according to the degree of difficulty these texts would have for "outsiders" (i.e., nonparticipants) who nonetheless have an interest in processing them. Generally, the linguistic difficulty inherent in a text will be approximately the same for both participants and nonparticipants, but there are some important exceptions to the rule. As I develop my ideas on text typology and processing, these points will be clarified.

Text Classification

In general, the simplest texts are those in which the information contained is bound up with facts, situations, and events outside the flow of language. As a result, these texts are often severely abbreviated, for it is assumed that the participant(s) will be guided by those externals. Thus, traffic and street signs, and for that matter signs of every type, are posted at physical locations which by their presence contribute to comprehension. In the case of recurrent situations and events (for example, greetings and farewells in daily conversation; pro forma information passed in communications dealing with plane landings and takeoffs; newspaper announcements of departures and arrivals of ships), the appropriate language use is directly linked to things outside the texts.

The participants in language events associated with level 1 will often be in a position to respond more quickly to language signals than nonparticipants. In pro forma situations where much of the information passed depends upon external factors, the users will obviously have inside knowledge and ways of discussing it not immediately accessible to outsiders. The latter will have to draw inferences about the information from other sources at their disposal or by accumulating data with the passage of time.

Language texts associated with level 2 are more demanding. They, too, are tied ultimately to the external world but are not dependent on immediate visual and auditory stimuli for their full interpretation. They are the products of speakers or writers who are conveying facts or exchanging information about situations and occurrences but are not analyzing or expressing personal involvement in the material conveyed. Such texts are based on the assumption that much of the information background is at least potentially shared in advance and the information itself will thus be easily internalized. As with level 1 texts, participants often fail to make explicit in conversation or letters things which they know as insiders. This means that nonparticipants must try to draw inferences regarding not only external clues but also other texts concerned with the same topics. (I should point out here that nonparticipants may have to draw on their analytic skills to cope with texts at *any* level of complexity and that the more complex the text, the less it will be resolvable from external clues.)

Texts associated with level 2 are more diverse in nature than level 1 texts. The latter, to be sure, show some variety in that they may relate to either static situations or dynamic events, but the grammar and lexicon are extremely restricted: synonymy of construction or vocabulary does not come into play. At level 2, though, the picture begins to change. Without the heavy dependence on perceptual clues from the outside and the resulting "one word–one perception" match, such language texts automatically reflect greater linguistic variety even though the participants are mainly communicating about factual things, with a minimum of analysis, commentary, or affective response. At level 2, speakers and writers have more occasion to make statements or give instructions than at level 1, where mere factuality is the main linguistic issue. A consequence of this is that any discourse or verbal exchange in a level 2 framework is bound to contain substitutable constructions and vocabulary items, even when by definition the topic is straightforward and at least partially shared. Thus, no two people would describe an accident in exactly the same way, even though all the details were clear and there was nothing extraordinary about the mishap itself, nor would they be likely to give accounts of a state visit in identical language. However predictable the event or transparent the facts, the code in which they are conveyed permits a fair variety of choice of expression.

Noncontrived level 2 texts represent the learner's initial exposure to linguistic discourse not keyed directly to the external environment. Hence, they are the first true linguistic challenge to the person who may have learned to make do by using (or at least recognizing) a combination of stock phrases and extralinguistic signs. The learner must now master a system in which linguistic units of various lengths may be substituted for, reordered in text, or even dropped, according to the rules of the language. In other words, the learner must master the basic rules of syntax.

At level 3, texts are more complex and require more of participants and nonparticipants alike. The difficulties of syntax are frequently compounded, and the lexicon is much more extensive so as to accommodate the need for highly analytic, as well as personalized, expression. Level 3 is the level at which language users respond intellectually, intuitively, or even instinctively, to the facts, situations, and events stated or narrated at level 2. Just as level 2 texts are qualitatively different from level 1 texts from a syntactic point of view, so level 3 texts make greater conceptual demands and consequently require a larger lexicon. Such control involves not only the degree of articulateness of the speaker(s)/writer(s) but also the partial internalization of another culture. Conceding that the facts or situations are perceived and reported in roughly the same way in two languages (a concession that may not be justifiable when the cultures differ widely), the responses to them are almost sure to be unpredictable to the cultural outsider. For example, an editorial (usually a perfect example for level 3 texts), containing a set of value judgments and responses, requires more effort to generate or to follow, as the case may be, than does a factual report. True as this undoubtedly is when the native language only is concerned, it is even more valid in the case of a second language (and culture). The one factor which may make level 3 texts relatively accessible is mutual knowledge of background events or circumstances contributing to the texts. Without that, the language user (frequently in nonparticipant status) may have an extremely difficult time in reconstructing the contributory data and, hence, in understanding the text.

The most difficult kind of text is associated with level 4. Unfortunately, both ILR and ACTFL/ETS statements on the level 4 skills are not as thoroughly developed as they might be, so the following description of level 4 texts is best understood in terms of the textual scale presented here, tentative as it may be.

It seems to me that the hallmark of these texts—the most difficult to access in the system—is the relative lack of shared information and assumptions. This is a function of a novel or creative approach to rethinking and verbalizing solutions to problems hitherto treated in a different way, or not at all. An example would be a "think piece" on the op-ed page of a newspaper or in a journal on the need to reformulate social, economic, or political policy on *X, Y* or *Z.*

Texts at this level presume little shared background or information; in other words, the writer or speaker is breaking new ground and hence must be explicit in his or her argumentation regardless of how abstract the material may be. Therefore, both participant and nonparticipant are on relatively the same footing in developing or reaching an understanding of these texts.

Text Classification Within Skill Levels

The descriptions above are meant to establish a scale graduated according to textual difficulty, which is in turn determined, at least in part, by the degree of shared information. These descriptions are, in other words, only intended to provide a skeleton in which the major structure is visible. Of course, this entails an element of oversimplification partially correctable by providing additional kinds of textual examples and by distinguishing levels within texts, particularly longer ones. I will now go over the territory again, introducing additional types of texts at each level (except at level 1, where the examples already given are fairly inclusive), explaining my rationale for assigning text *X* to level *Y,* and suggesting methods for testing language proficiency using the results of my analysis as guidelines.

In grouping texts at the four levels, I employ the term *mode* in the generalizing process. The word as I use it is not philosophically rigorous; it is meant to convey in a loose sense the way or manner in which language texts can be judged according to their evident purposes.

The Orientation Mode. First, I will consider the various kinds of texts at level 1. Whether these concern the identification of places and persons or the phase of activity, they have in common the purpose of orienting all concerned regarding who or what is where, or what is happening or supposed to happen within a generally predetermined pattern, much of which is external to language. I therefore assign level 1 texts to what I will call the *orientation mode.* As I pointed out earlier in the chapter, the language of such texts is extremely simple and, because of the one-to-one relationship of language and content at this level, the learner can control the material by understanding the content and memorizing in advance what language strings are likely or certain to occur. It is true, of course, that what begins as a routine rerun of a cyclical activity can suddenly become quite complex, with resulting problems for the analyst operating at level 1, or that a person asking for directions from a memorized formula can be swept away by a torrent of language at level 2 or higher. This fact, however, merely reflects the limitations of the individual operating only with memorized strings and proves that minimum working proficiency (i.e., level 2) requires skill at manipulating shorter strings in producing longer ones according to the rules of the particular language.

Test construction at level 1 should therefore center on problems of relevant content and not on language form (i.e., syntax). To be sure, particular language learners may acquire skills over different time periods: one learner may "top out" at level 1, while another is moving quickly through that learning phase toward level 2. However, if texts, whether produced or understood, are to drive the system (as I believe they must for proficiency testing and task assignment), ideally they should be tested in their own terms.

The Instructive Mode. Level 2 texts were exemplified earlier with reference to factual reports of the news-item variety. Actually, though, texts at this level may be rationalized to include a variety of other forms, such as extended instructions on how to assemble objects or complicated directions to remote places; recounting of incidents in one's past; narration of historical events; certain kinds of material where a supposedly factual treatment is strongly influenced by political theory; and, in speaking situations, exchanges of facts and opinions, and questions which elicit these (without, of course, statements of support of justification). These examples are incomplete in terms of the universe of level 2 discourse, but they have a common bond which permits their grouping under what I term the *instructive mode.*

As the term suggests, texts in this mode convey information about something that exists or is developing or should take place in the real world. They do not offer, as I have already noted, analytical or intuitive judgments concerned with this information. The varieties of language covered by this mode are far more numerous and harder to compare internally than those in the orientation mode. Thus, while it has been possible in government to distinguish operationally between level 1 and level 2 or level 2 and level 3, we have only just begun to order the varieties of texts *within* level 2. Therefore, to ensure that subjects are properly tested for the entire range of level 2, testers should either select one fairly long passage with a proper mixture of topic statements, amplifying statements, and (possibly) background detail; or they should choose a variety of texts most likely to give adequate coverage.

The Evaluative Mode. To level 3, I assign texts of every kind in which analysis and evaluation of things and events take place against a backdrop of shared information. These include editorials on and analyses of facts and events; apologia; certain kinds of belles-lettristic material, such as biography with some critical interpretation; and in verbal exchanges, extended outbursts (rhapsody, diatribe, etc.). These various forms may have little in common on the surface, but they do presume, as observed, a set of facts or a frame of reference shared by originator and receptor against which to evaluate what is said or written. I have chosen the term *evaluative mode* for the set of level 3 texts, even though *evaluative* may be wide of the mark as a label for certain kinds of affective language found in colloquial texts at this level.

As with level 2 texts, we have so far not attempted a rigorous graduation of textual subtypes within this level. In fact, we have not even come up with a tentative scale; so, again, test constructors should select for this level a variety of texts which will include analytic as well as affective language if they wish to cover the range of level 3.

The Projective Mode. Finally, I come to level 4, the most difficult level both in regard to setting the bounds of language use and describing the kinds of texts to be generated or understood.

Level 4, as I conceive it, is the level of language activity at which shared information and assumptions are at a minimum and personal input is paramount. Hence the texts which are generated and understood are highly individualized and make the greatest demands of the reader, a situation that immediately suggests literary creativity. Literary texts are indeed a hallmark of level 4 because they are uniquely the product of the individual with artistic bent. However, that level is not completely (or for that matter mostly) concerned with the esthetic. Linguistic production at level 4 involves an innovative approach to whatever topic the speaker/writer addresses, which in turn means that the received wisdom and methods of verbalizing it typical of other levels are found here only to the extent that they apply to the entire human race or to Western society or to some other large aggregate. These various highly individualized texts, in addition to belles-lettristic material and to the "think piece" cited earlier, include philosophical discourse, certain kinds of technical papers in which the facts and assumptions governing the field may be challenged or modified, and doubtless other forms of analysis or argumentation.

Level 4 texts as described above are rarely encountered in the colloquial language of exchange and are, in fact, infrequent even in the written language of daily commerce. However, there *are* texts of a colloquial nature which can be assigned to the *projective mode.* By definition, of course, they are highly individualized: while they do not make serious esthetic or intellectual demands of the reader/listener, they are relatively inaccessible either because they reflect unfamiliar cultural values or highly idiosyncratic language behavior or a combination of the two. Examples would include exchanges between thoughtful people as they address, or reconsider, personal problems or goals; discuss the merits of a work of art or a performance from personal perspectives; or merely give voice to private feelings.

Because of the individualized nature of level 4 texts, it is not surprising that skill statements for level 4 are ill defined and that guidance for test developers is virtually lacking. Nonetheless, texts do exist in every language at level 4; almost by definition they are culture-bound to the point of requiring an enormous effort by the learner; and sooner or later, the learner will be face-to-face with them. Therefore, theoretical and applied work is badly needed for test development at this level.

Some Unanswered Questions

I have not specifically addressed the following three questions: nonuniformity of level in some texts, subject matter issues, and the relationship of particular formal structures to texts at any level. Before closing, I will touch on them briefly.

As for the first question, texts may often reflect several levels, especially where some variety of the spoken language is involved. For example, at a press conference a news reporter may pose a straightforward question on, say, the possibility of a state visit from a foreign dignitary (level 2) and receive at the outset a reply in level 2 language, followed by level 3 language, as certain sensitive diplomatic issues are raised and then skirted. In a formal written text, an author may write an introduction in which he states circumstances which have prevailed in his domain (level 2) and comments on the need for rethinking the pertinent issues (level 3). He then may propose an entirely new approach to the problem in which received values are no longer valid (level 4).

In such cases, test constructors must select certain portions of the text, edit some stretches, or reject the text as unsuitable, depending on the known capability of the examinee, the pressure of circumstances, and so forth. Since texts can generally be found at the desired level if the testers work at it, this course should generally be followed.

On the question of subject matter, or text content, as a text issue, it hardly needs saying that some kind of subject matter is always present: language is not synonymous with syntax. From this it follows that shared facts and assumptions will play a role, no matter how general or technical the text may be. Unless there is an urgent need to test individuals in the narrow purview of a technical or scientific subject, such specialized material ought to be avoided: very often expert knowledge of a field can supply a form of semantic "feedback" into a text, so that test subjects may appear to know the foreign language better than they actually do. On the other hand, unfamiliarity with the subject matter may nonplus an examinee who otherwise knows the language concerned very well.

This in turn suggests question three: the relation of formal structures (i.e., syntax) to texts at the various levels. Syntax involves three considerations: classes of linguistic forms (e.g., nouns, verbs, pronouns), the order in which these appear in texts, and the intonational patterns (or, in the written language, the punctuation patterns) associated with them. For a language to be a language, rules governing these must be inferable from the outside, even though we cannot look directly into the brain to determine how they shape individual language behavior. Every language has its own version, or encoding, of these rules, which makes English, Chinese, and Russian what they are. The question then becomes: can we assign phrase, clause, and sentence types of levels in a systematic way? Unfortunately, the answer is no, even though it would make life easier if we could, for example, specify that conditional clauses are the distinguishing feature of level 3. However, we can point to trends or to high-frequency distributions according to which, for instance, simple imperative forms often appear at level 1: "ready, aim, fire!"; "stop!"; "to the rear march!" Similarly, declarative sentences without subordinate clauses are usual at level 2, especially in the simpler texts; conditional clauses are frequent at levels 3 and 4, although, as suggested, they cannot be used to characterize the levels as such. With more study in this area, we may be able to go farther in linking syntactic structures to texts, but I do not believe that text content can ever be superseded as the main discriminant in textual analysis.

To sum up, my aims in this paper have been to try to show that texts can provide a formal rationale for establishing skill levels, which so far have been stated only in operational form, and to suggest a classification for texts as the basis for testing. It is no more than a beginning, though I hope it is one on which further work can build.

5

Second Language Acquisition: Insights from a Proficiency Orientation

Heidi Byrnes
Georgetown University

The recent discussion of the meaning, indeed the appropriateness and even the advisability, of a proficiency orientation in second/foreign language (SL) teaching suggests the need for a critical look at the key issues (Savignon, 44; Hummel, 15; Lantolf and Frawley, 20). Although the concept of proficiency seemingly gained professional prominence through the back door, namely by serving as the conceptual framework for testing a learner's speaking abilities, the thrust of numerous presentations, intensive tester training and familiarization workshops, as well as publishing activity points to proficiency's potentially much wider application (Higgs, 11; James, 16). Questions arise regarding whether the insights gained from oral proficiency testing can and should affect syllabus design and curricular sequencing, what these insights might mean for materials development, and in a very cautionary way, what they might mean for classroom procedures and methodology.

Heidi Byrnes (Ph.D., Georgetown University) is Associate Professor of German at Georgetown University. She is a frequent presenter at professional meetings where her emphasis is on incorporating insights from linguistics and second language acquisition research into teaching practice. Her publications include *Contemporary Perceptions of Language: Interdisciplinary Dimensions,* published by Georgetown University Press; "Teaching for Proficiency: The Receptive Skills," in the 1985 *Northeast Conference Report*; and "Getting a Better Reading: Initiatives in Foreign Language Reading Instruction" in *Initiatives in Communicative Language Teaching II*. She is a certified tester and master trainer for the ACTFL/ETS method of assessing oral proficiency in German.

Author's note: I deeply acknowledge helpful comments on a draft version of this paper from a number of people: Michael Canale, Vicki Galloway, David Hiple, Pardee Lowe, Alice Omaggio, John Staczek, and Irene Thompson. And I am indebted to Michael Long's insights into SLA which stimulated me to write this paper in the first place. All remaining inaccuracies and inconsistencies are, of course, my own.

Obviously these issues have already generated a considerable amount of controversy, the raw material of vigorous debate for some time to come. That debate, I believe, will essentially remain circular or even vacuous unless we relate it to second language acquisition (SLA) research, particularly as SLA reports on instructed second language learning and, by extension, on SL teaching. The danger of yet another bandwagon, a danger conjured up by both proponents and opponents of a proficiency orientation, should make us think twice before we reach hasty conclusions about the various prescriptions already being offered by both sides.

The following discussion refers to insights gained through the ACTFL/ ETS procedure for assessing speaking proficiency in an oral interview, using the so-called academic scale currently set forth in the ACTFL Provisional Guidelines as the basis for assigning ratings. Published materials on implications and applications have steadily increased over the last few years and are readily available (Higgs, 11; James, 16; Omaggio, 37; *Die Unterrichtspraxis,* 8). Unfortunately, however, the interviewing and rating procedure itself and the many cautionary notes addressed to would-be testers during the intensive four-day workshop, as well as during the two follow-up phases of training, are not easily transmitted to the professional public as a whole. This situation in no way reflects any exclusivity, nor does it imply a diminished interest in open debate and clear statement of one's premises. It simply reflects a reality about how much of the art of interviewing can be transmitted in writing and how much must be observed and, consequently, can only be gained through practice. Most important, however, the experience of being involved in testing and, furthermore, in listening to significant amounts of live and taped speech produced by a wide variety of candidates gradually clarifies some initial professional hunches. Even so, this state of affairs does have the potential for leaving some published statements by proficiency advocates in a vacuum, and thus open to misinterpretation. Surely our profession needs no reminders that, as always in communicative interaction, the burden rests on both partners to act in good faith, to want to inform, and to want to understand.

In tracing the current misunderstandings, it is probably not incorrect to state that the sheltered existence oral proficiency testing led in government was not conducive to an elaborated theoretical framework. First developed over thirty years ago, it was an in-house tool that many people needed to learn to use effectively. The descriptors which gradually evolved for the ratings clearly betray the then-dominant structuralist viewpoint. We should also recall that, at the time, this approach incorporated a number of innovative features, such as criterion-referenced testing and Osgood's semantic differential. But, in retrospect, even these features proved inadequate for the current, more elaborated view of language. Thus, in the last years, since its arrival in academia, the testing procedure itself and its presuppositions have encountered greater scrutiny.

Today the need for an elaborated set of theoretical moorings can no longer be ignored. The profession as a whole has a right to know what is being advocated and what the theoretical implications are. I hasten to state that many of our perceptions are at this point rather vague, more like glimpses of possible directions than maps of clearly marked roadways. Hence, clarifying these perceptions assumes priority before we charge down dimly lit paths that offer scant chance of advancing our knowledge or even of an unscathed return.

By the same token the admission that the theoretical aspects of a proficiency orientation remain to be clarified is not particularly disturbing, as long as forthcoming clarification also offers an open invitation for bringing to bear on the issues pertinent knowledge about SLA and suggestions for future research directions. As a matter of fact, an honest assessment of the state of the art would show that, despite our best efforts and significant gains in the last fifteen years or so, little of what we know about SLA can truly lay claim to having uncovered causal relationships between input, whether naturalistic or instructed, and the learner's performance. Like it or not, only that causal relationship should compel us to change our ways of teaching.

Clearly we have not observed this rule in the past. On the contrary, it is precisely this lack of hard evidence, reinforced by our perplexing noninsistence on such evidence, which has made our field so prone to recurring cycles of prescriptions, either in the area of syllabus design (i.e., grammar-translation, structural, functional/notional, structural-functional, communicative) or in the area of methods (i.e., audiolingual, the Natural Approach, Silent Way, Suggestopaedia, etc.; see Richards, 42; Long, 26). In many cases little more than an intuitively appealing pronouncement was made, whose often poorly defined claims did not lend themselves or were never subjected to rigorous attempts at falsification, such as through more general evaluative procedures or through highly targeted classroom SLA research. For example, despite their appeal we have gleaned only meager knowledge about whether, how, and why communicative teaching approaches within a so-called communicative syllabus are more effective at helping learners acquire a second language as compared with, for example, audiolingual methods applied to a structural syllabus. At least with the latter, one can see a certain fit between syllabus and methodology; while with some more recent approaches not even that supportive relationship is revealed. Likewise the designation that there is a "natural" way to SLA suggests that all else is "unnatural" and, by extension, that people so persuaded need not further support their claims of success. At least the proficiency orientation furnishes us with an evaluative measure from the start against which any claims for syllabus and curriculum design or teaching methods can be compared.

As must be clear by now, I regard my remarks as part of an obligation to explore proficiency in depth on the part of those favorably inclined toward a proficiency orientation and its potential for enhancing SLA and SL teaching.

I approach the task of relating SLA theory to proficiency under three major headings: (1) assumptions inherent in the Oral Interview (OI) as a global assessment procedure; (2) insights into SLA that seem to present themselves in conjunction with the language evidence obtained in the OI; and (3) methodological and curricular implications. Interwoven are issues that have received special attention, such as the place of accuracy, the charge of elitism, the ultimate level of attainment and fossilization, and the relationship of proficiency to communicative competence. I close with brief comments about the role of teachers in a proficiency orientation.

The Oral Interview as a Global Assessment Procedure ___

The global assessment of oral proficiency (Lowe, 29) through the oral interview (OI) is based on key assumptions about language in general, about testing language use, and about SLA.

To grapple with the infinite possibilities that characterize language use, it is convenient to observe that use under three major categories: (1) the communicative tasks being performed; (2) the settings, both linguistic and nonlinguistic, which have given rise to and which support this communicative exchange; and (3) the felicity, or at least appropriateness, of the means being employed which facilitate for interlocutors the creation of meanings. Clearly language is not the only aspect of this complex process, nor is language necessarily and at all times the most prominent one. Should language gain such a status, it will do so only because of its ability to further nonlinguistic purposes, goals, and tasks. In other words, unless one continues to observe the mediating quality of language which is supported by a language group's total network of social interactions, one will, at best, observe peripherals and, at worst, proclaim fallacies about language.

The rating procedure for the OI captures task orientation of language under the concept of "function"; the interrelatedness of any task to a specific topic in a given setting falls under the heading "content/context"; and the success with which meaning is conveyed is categorized under "accuracy." It should be noted that "function" here does not refer to the seemingly endless array of functions in a functional/notional syllabus (Van Ek, 49; Munby, 35). Rather, function addresses broad task universals, such as the ability to create with the language in order to be able to give information of a personal nature or to solve some of the basic tasks of life in a given culture, the ability to narrate and describe in different time frames, and the ability to support an opinion on an abstract topic in detail. The second category of content/context seems rather straightforward. It refers to broad topical areas and the settings in which they can be dealt with, such as the ability to give background personal information or to participate in a professional discussion. However, it is the place of accuracy that has probably caused the greatest degree of misunderstanding and controversy (Savignon, 44; Lantolf and Frawley, 20).

Typically, accuracy is equated with knowledge of grammar, very much in the structuralist tradition. However, in the OI this category includes a number of factors—namely pronunciation, vocabulary, fluency, sociolinguistics/culture, and finally grammar—each one contributing in different amounts to the overall performance, depending on the speaker's proficiency level. For example, initially pronunciation and vocabulary might be most supportive of any communication occurring at all. However, at the higher levels, where we are concerned with excluding possible miscommunication rather than being satisfied with communication taking place at all, features of grammatical accuracy are likely to play a decisive role (Higgs, 12). In other words, the concern that proficiency signals a dangerous return to audiolingualism's emphasis on grammatical features proves unfounded.

On the contrary, grammar is but one factor in one of the three major categories (function, content/context, accuracy) under which we can observe language use (Lowe, 30). Very likely the false equating of accuracy with grammar, coupled with an unawareness of the compensatory nature of the scale below the Superior level, contributed to vehement reactions against the role of accuracy. This compensatory nature within the definitional constraints of the major levels (Novice, Intermediate, Advanced, Superior) holds true anywhere below the Superior level. It has always been part and parcel of the living tradition in oral proficiency testing that communication can, and indeed does, take place in numerous ways and in no way requires full command of the L2 grammatical system. In fact, in his historical overview of proficiency testing at the FSI, Sollenberger (47) reminds his audience of the distinction between accuracy in terms of technical skill and effective communication, and the possible disparity between the two. Nevertheless, it is equally true that if one wishes to differentiate between speakers performing the same task with the same content in the same setting, then the person using language with a higher degree of grammatical accuracy will generally be judged more proficient, though, in itself, this judgment does not necessarily result in a rating at the next higher level of proficiency. As stated, noncompensatory rating procedures do not apply rigorously until the Superior level, a level of substantial ability which only very few L2 college majors achieve (Carroll, 4). Consequently, the charge that proficiency testing promotes an additive, discrete-point system of assessing language use which is hung up on grammar and uses grammar as an unrealistic and even elitist distinguisher between speakers proves simply inappropriate.

In this context we note another approach to assessing global second language proficiency in speaking and writing which uses T-unit analysis as a predictor due to its avoidance of subjective judgments and ease of scoring. The research concluded that, while the average length of T-units seems to measure L1 proficiency quite effectively, for L2 proficiency, the length of *error-free* T-units resulted in a more powerful measure. Larsen-Freeman (21) speculates that L2 learners seem "capable of producing T-units of some length before they can be said to have truly acquired the L2." This result again points to the merits of holistically assessing language proficiency and considering performance factors, among them control of grammar, differently at different points of the scale.

Even more than the presumed role of accuracy, it may have been the breadth of language usage comprised by the scale which has provoked a charge of elitism: from no functional ability in L2 to ability equivalent to that of an educated native speaker of the L2. Since the scale was originally devised to assess highly specialized, professional-level language usage in the government, the extent of the scale's spread should hardly have come as a surprise. It is true that academia may have fewer requirements for testing speakers at this level. But it, too, must distinguish between those who speak the L2 with fluency and ease (as long as only concrete topics in a large variety of contexts must be addressed appropriately) and those who, in addition, can discuss differentiated issues. For academia these might be the implications of a piece of literature, treated insightfully, extensively, and with proper cultural references and nuancing in the chosen lexicon. The former speaker might be a student who has spent a year in the L2 culture, while the latter speaker would be our hope for a graduate-level literature seminar. The fact that the second level of L2 proficiency is exceedingly difficult to attain in no way nullifies its validity as a point along the continuum of observable language behavior. The rarity of such ratings only gives proper recognition to a learner's achievement when proficiency exceeds the more commonplace communicative needs.

The charge of elitism, I suspect, does not arise because language professionals are unaware of the significant differences in proficiency between speakers. Instead, it reflects a deep-seated restrictiveness in much of the discussion of SLA. For example, several frequently cited concepts—namely those surrounding Krashen's theories of SLA, the natural order hypothesis, the monitor model, the input hypothesis, the affective filter, and the learning-acquisition distinction—poorly defined as they are, are predicated on beginning students. For example, for Krashen "learning" is only possible for "easy" grammar, presumably on the order of elements in his highly generalized morpheme studies (see Long, 23). Even if these hypotheses were verifiable without leading to circular argumentation, the more dangerous implicit assumption that the claims they entail hold true for the entire progression of learning a language has yet to be adequately addressed and is surely far from proven. In other words, while it is prudent to be aware of the realities of American second language instruction and not nurture indefensible expectations for our instructional efforts, such prudence, if applied to assessing language proficiency as a whole, can all too easily turn into a misguided populism depriving us of the opportunity to understand the *whole* picture in SLA (Lowe, 30). Recent work in SLA seems to bear out this suspicion; interesting research results that have an impact on all our efforts, whether in beginning or advanced levels of instruction, are currently being obtained precisely when the conditions favorable to *higher* levels of SL attainment are scrutinized, that is, when a less constricted view of language and, consequently, of learning a language is adopted.

Some Insights into SLA Obtainable from Proficiency Testing

I believe that some of the greatest benefits of the increasing work being undertaken in academia with oral proficiency testing may well lie beyond the areas that come to mind most readily, such as placement, syllabus scope and sequence, course and program evaluation, entry and exit requirements, and required proficiency levels of TAs or teachers. Rather I consider the most exciting aspect its potential for giving language practitioners a framework within which to observe and evaluate the development of second-language proficiency in their students.

Teachers are constantly assessing student performance. However, I would like to suggest that they look afresh, from a broader perspective, at what actually happens. They should pose not only the standard question which pertains to the direct relationship between the input provided by them in instruction and the output students are able to provide. This would still be a narrow achievement orientation or, under the best of circumstances, a proficiency-oriented achievement orientation. But when we take a global view of proficiency, we are investigating what an L2 speaker can "communicate accurately in whichever language modality is pertinent to the communicative requirements of the situation" (Larson and Jones, 22). At this stage we are dealing with the *key questions in SLA,* namely the processes involved, the acquisitional sequences that seem to be followed, the rate of acquisition and, finally, the ultimate attainment. In other words, the OI does not just result in a product—a rating—but in data on the learner's processes in language use and language learning. Thus, insights gained from proficiency testing have strong potential for leading us to fruitful hypotheses about SLA which can then be tested in carefully controlled, classroom-centered research (Long, 24). Not every teacher will become a researcher. Yet I am confident that the basic tenets of proficiency testing and particularly the observational skills it fosters will enhance teachers' understanding of their professional experiences.

The following comments offer only suggestions, based on my experience with proficiency testing.

Processes

To abstract from the product to the processes is likely to prove a treacherous endeavor. As Hatch (10) points out, the process perhaps can never be discovered in the surface materials, the data. Nevertheless, she does urge that a closer look at the data might take us a long way on our quest. The following are some of the directions I note.

The current *ACTFL Proficiency Guidelines* distinguish at the lower levels of the scale between memorized material and creative language behavior. Though memorization as such may no longer be favored in all teaching styles, the distinction does refer to a real difference in language processing. McLaughlin (31, 32) has chosen to see this difference in terms of information processing, whereby the learner initially must attend consciously to the numerous subskills involved in L2 language use, a requirement that severely restricts efficiency, quality, and quantity of processing. This short-term memory processing is eventually automatized, allowing a good deal of processing to be shifted to long-term memory. From there information can be accessed as a chunked whole as a result of developing schemata, plans, and operations. Such a model of SLA would seem to place great emphasis on practice and could potentially be likened to some of the behaviorist tenets in audiolingual methodology. By contrast, a concept that has become prominent in recent SLA research, that of interlanguage, reflects the Chomskian ideas of innateness and language universals while further developing his concept of the learner's creativity. To Chomsky, the learner did not contribute much to the "unfolding of the genetic program—language." In this viewpoint, however, SLA involves a creative process in which the learner constructs the grammar of the target language according to certain, possibly universal, principles of hypothesis-testing, with the result that the speech produced at certain stages resembles neither the underlying grammar of L1 nor the input of L2 (Felix, 9).

Proficiency testing may be able to provide insights about the validity and the interrelationship of both constructs. The information-processing viewpoint that could account for speech with no particular interference from the L1 except in pronunciation seems particularly convincing at the Novice-Low and Novice-Mid levels where we observe rather halting speech, but with relatively good overall accuracy for limited tasks. This accurate though restricted language use might reflect the storage capacities of short-term memory whose limitations seem to have been reached by Novice-Mid (Miller, 34). Beyond that we glimpse more and more a creative approach which may at first be dominated by unconsciously held generalizations about language on the basis of the L1. On the one hand, this means a quantitative as well as a qualitative increase in expressive capabilities, in communicative performance; on the other hand, this creative hypothesis-testing results in highly flawed performance from the standpoint of grammatical accuracy. It seems to me at this point that particularly Intermediate-Low and Intermediate-Mid speech of the ACTFL/ETS scale is characterized by the kinds of errors that Seliger (46) traces to L1 interference, as contrasted with the errors occurring at the advanced levels, which show a higher incidence of overgeneralization of the L2. Since the scale is not a linear but a threshold-level scale the Mid-level ratings (distinguished for Novice and Intermediate only) seem to show a certain smoothness, a consolidation of how the learner currently views language. This contrasts markedly with the relatively unstable, "turbulent" speech of the Plus ranges (Novice-High, Intermediate-High, Advanced-Plus) assigned to speakers who show significant advances in attempting the next higher level's tasks but with an inability to sustain that performance consistently. Further implications of Seliger's observations which are tied to different student behavioral profiles will be touched upon in the section dealing with classroom teaching.

But, beyond interference errors, Intermediate speakers as a whole display some of the most baffling language use, conceivably a reflection of the shift from strategies primarily based on L1 transfer to strategies that reflect increased hypothesis-testing on the basis of L2. This shifting base for the learner's hypotheses leads to a transitional interlanguage system which, under ideal conditions, continues to be destabilized toward the system underlying the target L2. This is not necessarily a direct path. Hence, as repeatedly pointed out in other contexts, speakers who increase their proficiency level, such as from Intermediate-Low to Intermediate-High, are in no way to be equated with speakers who steadily decrease their rates of grammatical flaws. What changes, however, are their communicative ability and the types of errors which are observed. For the Intermediate level, then, the more interesting question for SLA research is much more likely to be the type of interlanguage system one can infer from speech performance, not a given speaker's level of accuracy.

Research by Meisel (33) points to a similar distinction for the phenomenon of simplification. Taking simplification as possibly a universal strategy, also reflected in pidginization and foreigner talk, he differentiates between restrictive simplification and elaborative simplification. The former reduces the grammatical system in order to meet communicative needs, for example, by using infinitives or one generalized inflection instead of diverse inflected forms. The latter is an intermediate stage which represents an extension of an earlier system in the direction of the target L2, such as the use of "wrong" forms. This move may involve not only the acquisition of new rules but also a loss of some earlier forms of simplification. Meisel's understanding of the two as being qualitatively distinct can be seen from his surmising that restrictive simplification may be tied to fossilization, while elaborative simplification represents a transitory interlanguage stage.

Sequences

My brief remarks about processing types indirectly referred to sequencing. We have previously characterized the proficiency scale as one built on a hierarchy of task universals. Choosing a readily apparent interpretation already captured in T-unit analysis or mean length-of-utterance measurement, we can expect a gradual shift from simple to complex constructions. But again, I believe that scrutinizing the data obtainable from proficiency testing will lead us much closer to Pienemann's research results (40). His current work reiterates the findings of the ZISA research group in Germany (7) who, on the basis of longitudinal and cross-sectional studies, found that learners of German as a second language seemed to show a sequence of certain acquisitional stages which can be predicted on the basis of the processing complexity required for the corresponding structures. For example, for the study's Romance learners of German, the initial hypothesis about basic German sentence word order was SVO (= stage X), the canonical form. Subsequent stages are determined by successively greater distance in terms of processing difficulty from this canonical word order: X+1, adverb preposing; X+2, verb separation; X+3, inversion; etc.

The reader will undoubtedly note a superficial similarity to the concept of i+1 as Krashen's recommendation for comprehensible input which is the precondition for SLA. However, there are three crucial differences: (1) the ZISA group's claims are capable of being operationalized and therefore can be falsified through observation of SLA; (2) they are independently verifiable through psycholinguistic research with respect to the stages' psychological plausibility and "learnability" (Clahsen, 6); and (3) they can be made in advance of the learning process rather than as an after-the-fact statement. Research into the feature of "learnability" as tied to a hypothesized sequence of acquisitional stages is beginning to be conducted (Johnson, 17). It not only reports the basic validity of a developmental skeleton for SLA but is equally concerned about establishing the status of variational features which any observation of the language use of different learners must acknowledge. An initial hypothesis for such variation accounts for differences not in quantitative grammatical terms but in terms of the communicative intentions and the cognitive prerequisites each learner brings to the task (Clahsen, 6). Among these would be factors addressed by the integrative/instrumental motivation distinction, or factors pertaining to the learner's preferred cognitive style. Thus the entire acquisition process is seen in terms of psychological, social, and language-internal factors, a position that in no way contradicts the possibility of a strictly ordered sequence of developmental stages. However, as Clahsen points out, it does require us to abandon the concept of L2 acquisition as a simple linear process. Rather it should be seen as a bidimensional process in which major and comparatively overlapping developmental stages permit a broad range of variations that reflect individual strategies, depending on the learner's own psychosocial situation. Such strategies might allow one to separate two major learner groups—those that are rhetorically more expressive and those that are concerned with errors (Clahsen, 6). The end result would be the structural heterogeneity of learners' interlanguage as we actually observe.

Again, it seems that data from proficiency testing can provide information about the interrelationship between posited developmental stages and variational features. It can do so since, unlike most other testing procedures, it does not rely on syntactic descriptors but presupposes a task orientation which values and attempts to establish a speaker's overall communicative effectiveness. Only with that type of assessment tool can we hope to establish the variational features and the communicative functions they serve, in turn allowing us to monitor more accurately and perhaps ultimately influence SLA.

I am keenly aware that professionals sceptical of data obtained through OIs for assessing proficiency would surely object to their use as the basis of possible statements about SLA. In response I would offer three "assignments": (1) an investigation of the research foundations for extant SL classroom methodology; (2) a comparative analysis of the method of data gathering in current SLA research and the degree to which any significant potential for communicative intentionality on the part of the informant and communicative interaction between data gatherer and informant is maintained; and (3) the experience of observing or at least listening to ten interviews at different levels of proficiency. I am confident that the insights gained from these experiences would promote the research potential of data obtained through OIs, while at the same time invalidating characterizations of the procedure as an interrogation that puts the examinees "on the spot" as it requires them to produce certain grammatical constructions (Savignon, 44).

On the contrary, the OI, unlike other methods of testing, is an adaptive test during which the candidate's performance influences the direction the assessment procedure takes. Therefore, it permits maximal observation of the communicative strategies available to learners, and indirectly the processing strategies they employ, without placing them into unduly stressful situations. Depending on the answers one seeks, such rich qualitative data may prove just as valid as quantitative data laced with linear statistics and correlational statements.

To support this claim, let me briefly allude to a personal observation about German OIs in the proficiency range from Intermediate-Mid on up. I find that much of the awareness of the essential features of language use that trainers wish to impart about testing in the upper levels of the scale can be summarized in the following question: what is the speakers' ability to shift elements out of the basic canonical position, which their current interlanguage system hypothesizes for these elements, into other positions, with the intention of conveying different meanings? Singling out, within SLA, the place of the processing demands involved in element shifting not merely emphasizes the parallels between such relatively well-known word order permutations as verb bracketing, the construction of compound tenses, or such increasingly complex syntactic features as movement of adverbials or relativization across sentence boundaries. More important, it allows for combining under one concept overt grammatical features of the product, with subtle semantic intentions, presumably part of the process. In other words, shifted elements should be taken by the observer as signals for differentiated meanings whose expression reflects a hierarchy of processing capabilities. For example, such movements can signal the length of utterance with which a speaker wishes to fill a turn (sentence, paragraph, or discourse), distinguish between old and new, between important and less important specific information, among opening, continuance, and closure of a line of argumentation, between backgrounding and foregrounding, and between major overriding and minor supporting discourse structures. The relevance of this kind of processing ability as learners attain higher levels of L2 proficiency cannot be overestimated. It deserves a closer look, since its manifestations, its sequencing, and its speed and ultimate level of attainment can provide us important clues about what goes on in SLA.

Ultimate Attainment and Rate of Acquisition

As mentioned earlier, two crucial questions have received remarkably little professional attention, as attested to by the dearth of research. These questions are (1) what is the ultimate level of language proficiency instructed learners can hope to reach under a given set of conditions, and (2) in what length of time can a given attainment level reasonably be expected. No doubt those classroom teachers charged with instruction at the more advanced levels of language learning have developed their own hunches about what has proven to be a help or a hindrance in developing their students' skills. More often than not those analyses take on the quality of a recitation of the things that somehow were not done before they received the students, coupled with the resignation that it is now too late to reverse the trend. Obviously, language professionals need to obtain a better understanding of those factors that allow speedier advance and, presumably, a higher level of ultimate attainment.

On the government side, experiential data with the OI exist, suggesting a threshold level below which maxi-immersion programs offered in combination with formal instruction are minimally effective (Lowe, 30). SLA research in general also offers some first results which point to the importance of timing different conditions of exposure for success in second language learning, though all are exceedingly cautious about the conclusions that should be drawn from them. Nevertheless, their combined weight seems to justify the conclusion that SL instruction does not need to be relegated to the ancillary function of helping beginners get comprehensible input in the sheltered environment of the classroom, whereupon they should quickly be released into a natural environment because formal instruction contributes little of substance to their SLA. On the contrary, evidence from immersion projects and from research comparing naturalistic with instructed learners seems to point increasingly to the crucial importance of formal instruction if rate of acquisition and ultimate level of attainment are considered.

In one such study, Pica (39) found that differing conditions of acquiring a language are reflected in the language being produced. While she makes no causal claims for rate of acquisition or ultimate attainment in different language contexts (naturalistic, instruction-only, and mixed) but only observed interlanguage production, she does note that the interlanguage among the three groups differed significantly with respect to types of production errors. Interestingly, different conditions of exposure do not affect the accuracy order in which grammatical morphemes are produced, a fact which would speak for some sort of universal learner contribution to the order of acquisition. Instead, the primary effect of instruction seemed to be that it triggered oversuppliance of grammatical morphology on the part of the learners and inhibited the use of ungrammatical, though communicatively effective, constructions.

While Pica's study refrains from statements about further language development by her subjects, a doctoral dissertation by Pavesi (38) does address the issue of ultimate attainment. She compared the acquisition of relative clause formation by naturalistic acquirers of English residing in Scotland and by Italian school children learning English through instruction in their native country. Although all learners followed the same sequence of acquisition, which fits the hierarchy of accessibility postulated by Keenan and Comrie (19), the naturalistic acquirers stopped at level 4 of this progression, relative clause formation with the object of a preposition, while the instructed learners went on to learn the more marked features of the construction, genitive relativization and relativization of an object of comparison. Pavesi, too, is reluctant to deduce that explicit teaching of rules promotes the acquisition of a full inventory of language forms, whereas lack of it does not. Rather, she suggests that the deciding factor may lie in the different discoursal modes to which both groups were exposed, unplanned versus planned discourse, with the latter favoring the higher occurrence of the more marked forms of relativization. However, she does note that, in view of the disparity of amount of contact with the target language—the naturalistic acquirers had been in country for an average of six years—formal instruction did seem to result in a faster rate of acquisition.

Finally, increasing evidence from immersion projects, such as the numerous Canadian immersion projects and the Culver City Project in California, indicates that naturalistic acquirers in those surroundings fall short on a wide variety of morpho-syntactic constructions and, in fact, seem to be fossilizing in their language use (Campbell, 2; Swain, 48).

It is precisely this concern about an apparent halt in the destabilization of a learner's interlanguage system which Higgs and Clifford (13) address in an article whose conclusions have often been misrepresented as advocating a return to old-fashioned grammar teaching. The authors base their hypotheses about the relative contribution of skills to an overall rating on practical experience with proficiency testing and adduce the psychological construct of proactive interference as potentially explaining the observed phenomenon of fossilized incorrect grammatical patterns. This phenomenon is more likely to occur when students are regularly rewarded for linguistically inaccurate but communicatively appropriate performances. As the authors suggest, what is necessary is evidence from a longitudinal study controlling for the various types of input, naturalistic or instructed, and then comparing the language use of the respective groups. Such a study is currently being prepared at the University of Hawaii, investigating native Japanese speakers learning English and native speakers of English learning Japanese under four different conditions of exposure: (1) instruction only, (2) instruction followed by exposure, (3) exposure and instruction, and (4) exposure only (Long, 27).

Proficiency testing in the academic environment, combined with a detailed record about an examinee's previous language aptitude and experience, could provide further insights about the extent and type of exposure likely to prove most beneficial. One instance of the need to follow up exposure with high-level emphasis on form is reported by Véguez (50). Seniors at Middlebury College who in the previous year had participated in a study abroad program in an L2 university setting, presumably with sufficient exposure to the very kind of planned discourse Pavesi refers to, nevertheless had not acquired some high-level structural features of the language, a deficiency which became particularly evident in a writing course. In response, a newly devised course will focus precisely on some of these grammatical features. Its outcomes should prove significant.

In a recent article, Long (26) presents a similar argument. While the precise causes and the instructional ramifications to be drawn from the phenomena observed in the above studies are not conclusive, he speculates that emphasis on form may well turn out to be a key factor because of the possibility that classroom instruction may bring saliency to the targeted features. He, too, is quick to caution against an unthinking return to teaching discrete grammar points but looks to SLA research to help us determine just what such an instructional approach would entail. In the following, I will present some thoughts from a proficiency orientation.

Methodological and Curricular Implications of Proficiency

My remarks about the importance of, and indeed the necessity for, an elaborated research basis should make it clear that I find much in proficiency exciting and worthy of closer investigation. My hope is that, before too long, such efforts can provide specific recommendations for more effective SL teaching. However, I am convinced that we already possess valuable evidence that allows us to make some initial broad adjustments in our classrooms and in our programs without running the risk of propagating hastily conceived notions.

Clearly, the momentum among those in the profession who have gained familiarity with the concept of proficiency points in the direction of an application of the findings obtained through testing. This necessitates some caution. All of us, no matter what our theoretical persuasion, are aware that, just as there is no direct transfer of results from studies of L2 acquisition to the classroom, there is also no direct transfer from the results of proficiency testing to the classroom. Aside from having learned to acknowledge that SLA itself is not a linear process easily translatable into a linear course and curricular design, we must recognize additional mediating variables, such as the influence of instruction, of educational theory, of a host of student variables. For most of these factors we simply know too little to be able to formulate narrowly defined prescriptive statements.

Nevertheless, we should also bear in mind that causalities are extremely difficult to establish or, when established, have marginal significance for the practitioner. I believe that, as it stands, there are substantive noncontroversial findings which have come out of an association with proficiency whose implementation in teaching practice would significantly improve SL instruction. As a matter of fact, I am convinced that recommendations based on these findings in part echo points advocated previously, such as in a communicative teaching approach. The difference is that we can now substantiate claims made for them on the basis of testing evidence. And we can make their impact on SLA more immediate to teachers as they experience an insightful way of observing language use, their own, that of their students, and that of those who use the L2 in a natural setting.

The ability to observe language use in an acutely critical way is perhaps the most crucial benefit of the experience with proficiency and, to me, the results of that critical assessment form the central justification for any recommendations for classrooms and curricula. We must continually remind ourselves of our obligation to substantiate the insights from those observations through controlled research, but we should also not be afraid to speak out on some phenomena even now.

Discussed below are three such phenomena which have arisen in conjunction with the structure and the process of the OI: the role of the interviewer as communicative partner, the hierarchy of tasks implicit in the rating scale, and the role of the examinee/learner.

Methodological Insights from Proficiency Testing Itself

The Role of the Interviewer. Undoubtedly the most frequently mentioned and most difficult hurdle prospective testers must overcome is to learn to conduct a valid conversational exchange with their partner, one which does not focus on structural evidence but on an ability to communicate meanings successfully. For many testers the opportunity, available during the extensive training phase, to critically examine their own language use occasions the biggest initial shock as they learn the art of interviewing.

Often testers find that their language behavior bears little resemblance to normal conversations, with the feature most in need of attention being the types of questions they tend to pose. Since the goal of the OI is to obtain a ratable sample of speech, such that one can validly assess a speaker's ability to use language to perform a variety of tasks, the tester must in fact elicit communicatively valid tasks in a fashion that resembles a natural conversation as closely as circumstances of testing and the limitations of the interlocutor's language permit. The problematic characteristics of questions posed by novice testers during their first practice interviews are completely corroborated in a study by Long and Sato (28), who observed classroom discourse and compared this with natural native-speaker–nonnative-speaker (NS-NNS) conversations outside the classroom. They found that while display questions—questions where the information is already known—overwhelmingly dominated classroom conversation, they are virtually unknown in informal NS-NNS conversations. Conversely, information questions, which form the backbone of a natural conversation and of solid proficiency testing, represent a minute share of teachers' question inventories. Furthermore, teacher discourse shows a high incidence of statements, typically the feedback moves after student response, and a fair number of imperatives. Both of these features are much rarer in the NS performance. While imperatives obviously reflect the need for classroom management, the distorted proportion of display to referential questions is in no way motivated by the classroom setting or the limited proficiency of the students.

On the contrary, as Long and Sato (28) point out, "access to comprehensible input and opportunities to use the target language for communicative purposes are probably the minimum requirements for successful classroom SLA." Far too often classroom discourse follows the pattern of initiation, response, feedback. If, in addition, that initiation is a "test" or "known information" question, then the social and communicative validity of the entire exchange is suspect from the start. The student can hardly be said to have been given an opportunity for interaction. Such interaction centers around the communication of meanings; presupposes planning of a strategy of how to present one's message at each turn, as well as over the entire communicative exchange; involves uptake of the comments made by the conversational partner; and typically implies the negotiation of meanings through several turns. This inability to carry out a communicative plan has been pointed out as one of the hallmarks of instructed SL learners (Hüllen, 14). Essentially they remain reactive, perhaps even being deceivingly smooth in that behavior, but highly dependent on the teacher to break down an entire message into its component yes/no or display questions to which they only need to nod assent or disagreement or provide a highly restricted utterance.

The counterproductiveness of such student behavior, which is primarily controlled by the teacher, is only matched by its lack of justification from the standpoint of the classroom setting. Providing even more research support, Seliger (46) points to the importance of intensive classroom interaction to facilitate the evolution of a more mature error profile, one no longer restricted to intuitions from L1 but informed by the increasing opportunity to try out hypotheses on the basis of L2. For all levels of learners, such interaction need not be equated with so-called simplified language, which has potential difficulties of its own (Chaudron, 5); rather, it is marked by a different interactional structure, modified through such devices as repetition, rephrasing, and various forms of discourse repair and questioning (Long and Sato, 28).

In that connection Seliger presents a provocative analysis of teacher questions with respect to the degree to which an individual student feels a *need* to attend to the teacher's language. A need would be established if the teacher's question were a real and personalized one, such that a response involving meaning transfer, which only the individual student can accomplish, can reasonably be expected. Likewise, the degree to which students feel conversationally obligated to initiate an interaction depends on the degree to which they can expect an utterance to be properly attended to by the teacher. Both the conversational need for response and initiation activity constitute a significant indication of the amount of real communication taking place in the classroom. Aside from the humanistic value of according learners a status of equality as conversational partners, personalized input holds the greatest promise for enhancing an active learning style which, due to the opportunity for intensive and sustained hypothesis testing, would lead to a faster rate of SL acquisition.

On a related matter, the OI has demonstrated that, in general, teachers/ testers do not offer students the response time so crucial, even in native language tasks, for memory and the development of logical reasoning (Shrum, 45). For SL tasks we can assume that the increased processing demands present additional justification for longer waiting periods, particularly if thoughtful communication, and not just pattern-drill language, is the goal.

I trust that the discussion thus far is largely above controversy. Yet, experience with proficiency testing points to an astounding gap between what the vast majority of teachers, of a communicative bent or not, would intellectually accede to—even believe they are doing in their classrooms—and their teaching practices. It scarcely needs pointing out that the distance to the proposals by theoreticians, methodologists, and curriculum specialists is likely to be even greater, making the effectiveness of their pronouncements questionable. Unless we succeed in reaching classroom teachers and enable them, in the most immediate fashion possible, to gain a realization of the repercussions of their classroom language use, much of our professional discussion will remain idle talk. I do not wish to sound like an alarmist, but the pervasiveness of the teacher behaviors described above is such that consciousness-raising almost reaches proportions of reeducation, a process that, fortunately, can be monitored by the teachers themselves as they go through learning and practicing the art of interviewing. If the experience with proficiency testing would have no other effect than that of redirecting teachers' classroom discourse behaviors away from a preoccupation with form to meaning, from accuracy to communication, it would achieve a goal far more substantial than the typical knowledge goals of many a methods course.

The Hierarchy of Tasks: As indicated earlier, the rating scale is built around a postulated hierarchy of tasks. This implies that a substantial ability to perform effectively the tasks of a certain level must be observable in language use before we can assume efforts to handle the tasks of the next higher level. For instance, if a learner can produce simple biographical information, particularly when aided by the prodding questions of a sympathetic listener interested in knowing more, then it is unrealistic to expect that same speaker to be able to narrate past events in a detailed fashion or to explain the complex circumstances of an event with finesse. This does not mean that learners should be sheltered from more challenging tasks. However, it does mean that a sensitive teacher refrains from routinely expecting students to overextend their linguistic reach, with the threat of less than optimal learning alluded to by some of the cited SLA research. Instead, classroom instruction will first aim at consolidating students' skills by offering a wide variety of interactive tasks at the same proficiency level, exploring different situational contexts, and therefore involving lexical diversification in a meaningful fashion. In time, in an overlapping fashion, higher-level tasks can be incorporated, allowing for the kind of extensive exposure and opportunity for practice that we find ever more essential for the learners' gradual increase in accuracy that has been noted again and again by SLA researchers.

Task-Based Testing. Beyond its utility for globally assessing a learner's proficiency and for devising teaching strategies built around interactive tasks, a task-based approach to language has valid application possibilities for the kind of testing routinely conducted in all formal learning environments, namely, achievement testing. Much as classroom discourse at times is totally divorced from real discourse, so the kind of testing we conduct often has nothing to do with establishing whether a learner can perform real tasks. Even if the classroom discourse shows a communicative orientation, testing still reflects old habits. The traditional emphasis on form elements, together with a misconception about the scientific rigor to which classroom tests should adhere, has supported sterile formats from which the learner cannot help but deduce that learning and testing are totally unrelated activities. I am convinced that the experience of proficiency testing enhances a teacher's sensitivity to the principles and test design features recommended by Canale (3) whose main goal in advocating new approaches to testing is "to encourage and to exploit the intrinsic evaluation that characterizes any authentic language use and language learning," a crucial connection also upheld by Omaggio (36) in a discussion of language practice activities in the classroom and in testing.

Thus, from a proficiency viewpoint, both L2 learning and testing assign a vital role to the learner, one of active participation, of involvement and personal responsibility for goals and outcomes, all within a comprehensive framework for optimizing SLA.

Curricular Implications

Just as the methodological implications deriving from a proficiency orientation are at this point rather broadly defined, so, too, are the recommendations pertaining to curriculum. Again, their generality should not be confounded with superficiality or irrelevance, but should be taken as an indication of their applicability at all levels of instruction.

The first of these recommendations—namely, the implementation of the concept of accountability into our curricular structure—should come as no surprise. It is indeed remarkable how much of curriculum model-building has neglected to include a mechanism by which we can determine a program's rate of success. Accountability automatically involves the statement of goals, the tasks for reaching those goals, the selection and organization of curricular content, an indication of the learning theory and the methodology which would enhance attainment of the goals, and, finally, a mode of assessment. A proficiency orientation can contribute to all these steps in curriculum development.

Second, since the goal of proficiency is usable language, the most frequently advocated curricular progression focuses on learning tasks (Richards, 43; Long, 25). These should in some way incorporate a needs assessment reflecting the particular learner group. While it is impossible to detail specific proposals here, I would like to highlight what I see as their characteristic features.

Task-based learning in the context of proficiency assumes the existence of a task hierarchy. Such a hierarchy can be expressed in terms of continua along at least the following familiar lines (Byrnes, 1): (1) with respect to the amount of interaction required by the participants in conversation, i.e., the so-called survival situations vs. the situations with a complication which the OI includes; (2) with respect to the subject matter being discussed, i.e., concrete topics pertaining to the immediate situation, linguistic or nonlinguistic, as contrasted with topics more and more distant in time and place, progressing to abstract topics; (3) with respect to the speaker's primary communicative intention, i.e., solving mostly transactional tasks, or informing, narrating, describing, presenting an opinion, persuading, negotiating, etc.; and (4) with respect to the formal complexity of the language likely to be required for adequately performing the task, i.e., utterance length, and with it structural and lexical complexity, tending toward the word and phrasal level, the level of individual sentences, paragraphs, or extended discourse.

As far as SLA is concerned, all these parameters are assumed to interlock in a nonrandom fashion, allowing general specifications for tasks which in turn have an impact on curricular sequencing. Hence, in contrast to a naturalistic learning environment, the curricular arrangement of tasks in instructed SLA is not biased exclusively toward the frequency of occurrence of one task type over the other—although it would not be unreasonable to expect frequency to be an important factor in the learner's ability to master them. Instead, curricular sequencing must take into account the major developmental stages that SLA research is now beginning to identify. Simply put, they indicate that the likelihood of the learners' ability to acquire certain L2 uses is enhanced by an existing ability to perform tasks which have slightly lower processing demands.

Curricular sequencing with such a psycholinguistic basis would speak to one of the perceived shortcomings of the communicative approach. Although proponents of communicative competence insist on language use, an insistence akin to that in a proficiency orientation, little in their advocacy translates into an instructional sequence. Therefore, many communicative materials, particularly in the United States, continue to favor a grammatical progression. While in itself that is not an unreasonable approach, it is optimal only if the grammatical progression parallels a psycholinguistic progression of difficulty. Communicative language teaching, as generally practiced to date, has yet to establish that crucial correlation. Perhaps a proficiency orientation is better able to provide a framework within which to prove or disprove such a connection, to look for alternative modes of sequencing, and ultimately, to propose an enhanced syllabus.

The concerns for more effective syllabus design are succinctly summarized by Pienemann (40, 41) in the concepts of learnability and teachability. He maintains that (1) every learner builds up his or her own grammar, (2) you cannot teach everything you want, (3) premature learning is counterproductive, and (4) teaching must be learnable. Underlying these statements is a view of the language learning process that assumes certain processing constraints which are a decisive cause for the specific order in which L2 features are being acquired. As noted earlier, positing acquisitional stages leaves sufficient room for individual variation; but for teaching to become more efficient, one must first diagnose the learner's current acquisitional stage and predict from it the subsequent one. Since these orders derive from observation of use, they would not in themselves give us a blueprint for action in the classroom. Nevertheless, they furnish us an indication of the *direction* we should be following in order to be more effective.

It is this kind of narrowing-down of the acquisitional stages that proficiency makes possible for the practitioner. We are at stage A, which has certain characteristics that are processing prerequisites for the subsequent stage B. We seek to reach stage B, which has another, not unrelated, set of characteristics. What available knowledge can we bring to bear on choosing an instructional format that would not only build on the psycholinguistically natural progression but also accelerate it? In other words, instead of instruction being the stepchild to naturalistic acquisition as much of recent methodology has proclaimed it to be, Pienemann sees a potential for amending this "'deficient' acquisition process through systematic formal instruction."

I am convinced that, for those who have familiarized themselves with a proficiency orientation, a significant part of its appeal, resulting in the enthusiasm with which they have embraced it, lies precisely in its potential for guiding their professional efforts constructively rather than denying their validity altogether or relegating them to marginal status.

It would be fallacious to claim that the major levels of the proficiency scale directly relate to the processing stages Pienemann refers to. Indeed, that topic would be well worth investigating. Nevertheless, the concepts of learnability and teachability have already seen successful application within the proficiency orientation (Kaplan, 18). While the corollary, that premature teaching is counterproductive, has to my knowledge not yet been formally investigated by proficiency advocates, we surely have much indirect evidence, though no hard data, from the many proficiency tests that have been administered to learners who clearly did not maximally benefit from the instruction they received. Perhaps mutually supportive research into both areas, the learnability and the nonlearnability of certain structures at certain stages, would hold the promise for helping us overcome the vexing problem of fossilization of concern to us all.

Having dwelt at length on the relatively fixed developmental features of an interlanguage, I would like to close with a few thoughts on variational features. Their membership and their causes are theoretically less well defined. Learner variables that take into account the degree of willingness to become integrated into the L2 culture may have sufficient explanatory validity for natural acquisition, but they would seem to hold less promise in a formal L2 learning environment. We have already mentioned that the kind of input may favorably influence the accuracy of a given form in learners' interlanguage; we have also referred to different discourse modes as potentially affecting ultimate attainment; and we have emphasized the value of interactive classrooms to help students obtain larger amounts of input on which to build their hypotheses about the L2. All these recommendations refer either to learner variables that teachers may have little control over or to variables that pertain to the kind of language being used by teachers and the purposes for which it is used in the classroom, perhaps traditionally the touchiest issue. While it would be unwise to expect drastic changes in classroom procedures, I would like to express the hope that teachers who have experience with the premises of proficiency testing are likely to view language not only as form but also as function, not only as product but also as process, and as a creative, interactive task performance rather than as an uncontextualized set of linguistic behaviors.

The more these insights can be experientially based, as proficiency testing is able to make them, the more teachers will be inclined to let them affect their instructional approach. I suggest that, ultimately, it will be those changes, supported by curricular design and materials development, which will facilitate positive results in instructed SLA. As much as possible teachers should be aware of the many processes their students invoke as they produce language. Yet, it is not essential for them to know what linguists, under the concept of "competence," represent as language knowledge. In the end, such representations may have little to do with the language user's knowledge. Instead, teachers would be better able to accomplish what they set out to do—namely, to enhance their students' chances to reach the highest level of proficiency attainable under the circumstances. For, while a competence-oriented approach, even if we could define it more clearly, does not necessarily result in performance, an underlying communicative competence does gradually develop as a necessary part of a proficiency/performance approach. If, in addition, these efforts should spark an SLA research interest, then proficiency would, in fact, become the organizing principle its proponents suggest it is.

References, Second Language Acquisition: Insights from a Proficiency Orientation

1. Byrnes, Heidi. "Grammar—Communicative Competence—Functions/ Notions: Implications for and from a Proficiency Orientation." *Die Unterrichtspraxis* 17, 2 (1984):194–206.
2. Campbell, Russell. "Variations on the Immersion Model of Foreign Language Education." Paper presented at the Georgetown University Round Table on Languages and Linguistics, June 27–29, 1985.

3. Canale, Michael. "Language Assessment: The Method Is the Message," pp. 249–262 in Deborah Tannen and James E. Alatis, eds., *Languages and Linguistics: The Interdependence of Theory, Data, and Application* (GURT 1985). Washington, D.C.: Georgetown University Press, 1986.
4. Carroll, John B., et al. *The Foreign Language Attainments of Language Majors in the Senior Year: A Survey Conducted in U.S. Colleges and Universities.* Cambridge, MA: Graduate School of Education, Harvard University, 1967. (EDRS:ED 013 343)
5. Chaudron, Craig. "Foreigner Talk in the Classroom—An Aid to Learning?" pp. 127–43 in Herbert W. Seliger and Michael H. Long, eds., *Classroom Oriented Research in Second Language Acquisition.* Rowley, MA: Newbury House, 1983.
6. Clahsen, Harald. "Psycholinguistic Aspects of L2 Acquisition," pp. 57–79 in Sascha Felix, ed., *Second Language Development: Trends and Issues.* Tübingen: Gunter Narr, 1980.
7. _____; Jürgen Meisel; and Manfred Pienemann. *Deutsch als Zweitsprache. Der Spracherwerb ausländischer Arbeiter.* Tübingen: Gunter Narr, 1983.
8. *Die Unterrichtspraxis* 17, 2 (1984).
9. Felix, Sascha, ed. *Second Language Development: Trends and Issues.* Tübingen: Gunter Narr, 1980.
10. Hatch, Evelyn. "Second Language Acquisition—Avoiding the Question," pp. 177–83 in Sascha Felix, ed., *Second Language Development: Trends and Issues.* Tübingen: Gunter Narr, 1980.
11. Higgs, Theodore V., ed., *Teaching for Proficiency, the Organizing Principle.* The ACTFL Foreign Language Education Series. Lincolnwood, IL: National Textbook Co., 1984.
12. _____. "Teaching Grammar for Proficiency." *Foreign Language Annals* 18, 4 (1985):289–96.
13. _____, and Ray Clifford. "The Push toward Communication," pp. 57–79 in Theodore V. Higgs, ed., *Curriculum, Competence, and the Foreign Language Teacher.* The ACTFL Foreign Language Education Series. Lincolnwood, IL: National Textbook Co., 1982.
14. Hüllen, Werner. "Investigations into Classroom Discourse." Paper presented at the symposium, Current Trends in European Second Language Acquisition Research. Georgetown University, July 27–28, 1985.
15. Hummel, Robert D. "Evaluating Proficiency in Comprehension Skills: How Can We Measure What We Can't Observe?" *ADFL Bulletin* 16, 2 (1985):13–16.
16. James, Charles J., ed. *Foreign Language Proficiency in the Classroom and Beyond.* The ACTFL Foreign Language Education Series. Lincolnwood, IL: National Textbook Co., 1985.
17. Johnston, M. "Self-Directed Learning and ESL Development." Adult Migrant Education Service, N.S.W. Australia. MS, 1984.
18. Kaplan, Isabelle M. "Oral Proficiency Testing and the Language Curriculum: Two Experiments in Curricular Design for Conversation Courses." *Foreign Language Annals* 17, 5 (1984):491–97.
19. Keenan, Edward L., and Bernard Comrie. "Noun Phrase Accessibility and Universal Grammar." *Linguistic Inquiry* 1 (1977):63–99.
20. Lantolf, James P., and William Frawley. "Oral-Proficiency Testing: A Critical Analysis." *Modern Language Journal* 69, 4 (1985):337–45.
21. Larsen-Freeman, Diane. "Assessing Global Second Language Proficiency," pp. 287–304 in Herbert W. Seliger and Michael H. Long, eds., *Classroom Oriented Research in Second Language Acquisition.* Rowley, MA: Newbury House, 1983.

22. Larson, Jerry W., and Randall L. Jones. "Proficiency Testing for the Other Language Modalities," pp. 113–38 in Theodore V. Higgs, ed., *Teaching for Proficiency, the Organizing Principle.* The ACTFL Foreign Language Education Series. Lincolnwood, IL: National Textbook Co., 1984.

23. Long, Michael H. "Does Second Language Instruction Make a Difference? A Review of Research." *TESOL Quarterly* 17, 3 (1983):359–82.

24. _____. "Training the Second Language Teacher as Classroom Researcher," pp. 281–97 in James E. Alatis, H. H. Stern, and Peter Strevens, eds., *Applied Linguistics and the Preparation of Second Language Teachers: Toward a Rationale.* Washington, D.C.: Georgetown University Press, GURT 1983.

25. _____. "A Role for Instruction in Second Language Acquisition: Task-based Language Teaching," pp. 77–99 in Kenneth Hyltenstam and Manfred Pienemann, eds., *Modelling and Assessing Second Language Acquisition.* Clevedon, Avon: Multilingual Matters, 1985.

26. _____. "Instructed Interlanguage Development," in Leslie Beebe, ed., *Issues in Second Language Acquisition: Multiple Perspectives.* Rowley, MA: Newbury House, in press.

27. _____. Class discussion during the course, Second Language Acquisition, at the LSA/TESOL Institute held at Georgetown University, June 24–August 2, 1985.

28. _____, and Charlene J. Sato. "Classroom Foreigner Talk Discourse: Forms and Functions of Teachers' Questions," pp. 268–85 in Herbert W. Seliger and Michael H. Long, eds., *Classroom Oriented Research in Second Language Acquisition.* Rowley, MA: Newbury House, 1983.

29. Lowe, Pardee, Jr. "The ILR Oral Interview: Origins, Applications, Pitfalls and Implications." *Die Unterrichtspraxis* 16, 2 (1983):230–44.

30. _____. "The ILR Proficiency Scale as a Synthesizing Research Principle: The View from the Mountain," pp. 9–53 in Charles J. James, ed., *Foreign Language Proficiency in the Classroom and Beyond.* The ACTFL Foreign Language Education Series. Lincolnwood, IL: National Textbook Co., 1985.

31. McLaughlin, Barry. "The Monitor Model: Some Methodological Considerations." *Language Learning* 18, 2 (1979):309–32.

32. _____; Tammy Rossman; and Beverly McLeod. "Second Language Learning: An Information-Processing Perspective." *Language Learning* 33, 2 (1983): 135–58.

33. Meisel, Jürgen M. "Linguistic Simplification," pp. 13–40 in Sascha Felix, ed., *Second Language Development: Trends and Issues.* Tübingen: Gunter Narr, 1980.

34. Miller, C. A. "The Magical Number Seven, Plus or Minus Two: Some Limits on Our Capacity for Processing Information." *Psychological Review* 63 (1956):81–97.

35. Munby, John. *Communicative Syllabus Design.* Cambridge: Cambridge University Press, 1978.

36. Omaggio, Alice C. *Proficiency-Oriented Classroom Testing.* Washington, D.C.: Center for Applied Linguistics, 1983.

37. _____, ed. *Proficiency, Curriculum, Articulation: The Ties That Bind.* Middlebury, VT: The Northeast Conference, 1985.

38. Pavesi, Maria. "Linguistic Markedness, Discoursal Models, and Relative Clause Formation in a Formal and an Informal Context." Paper presented at the IRAAL-BAAL Seminar on Formal and Informal Contexts of Language Learning. Dublin, Ireland, September 11–13, 1984.

39. Pica, Teresa. "Adult Acquisition of English as a Second Language under Different Conditions of Exposure." *Language Learning* 33, 4 (1983):465–97.

40. Pienemann, Manfred. "Psycholinguistic Principles of Second Language

Teaching." Revised version of a paper given at the National Australian TESOL Conference, Melbourne, June 1984.

41. _____. "Psychological Constraints on the Teachability of Languages." *Studies in Second Language Acquisition* 6, 2 (1984):186–214.

42. Richards, Jack C. "The Secret Life of Methods." *TESOL Quarterly* 18, 1 (1984):7–23.

43. _____. "Planning for Proficiency." Plenary address given at the CATESOL Convention in San Diego, CA, April 19–21, 1985.

44. Savignon, Sandra J. "Evaluation of Communicative Competence: The ACTFL Provisional Proficiency Guidelines." *Modern Language Journal* 69, 2 (1985):129–34.

45. Shrum, Judith L. "Wait-time and the Use of Target or Native Languages." *Foreign Language Annals* 18, 2 (1985):305–13.

46. Seliger, Herbert W. "Learner Interaction in the Classroom and Its Effects on Language Acquisition," pp. 246–66 in Herbert W. Seliger and Michael H. Long, eds., *Classroom Oriented Research in Second Language Acquisition.* Rowley, MA: Newbury House, 1983.

47. Sollenberger, Howard E. "Development and Current Use of the FSI Oral Interview Test," pp. 3–12 in John L. D. Clark, ed., *Direct Testing of Speaking Proficiency.* Princeton, NJ: Educational Testing Service, 1978.

48. Swain, Merrill. "Communicative Competence: Some Roles of Comprehensible Input and Comprehensible Output in Its Development," pp. 235–53 in Susan M. Gass and Carolyn G. Madden, eds., *Input and Second Language Acquisition.* Rowley, MA: Newbury House, 1985.

49. Van Ek, Jan, ed. *Threshold Level English.* Oxford: Pergamon Press, 1980.

50. Véguez, Roberto. "The Oral Proficiency Interview and the Junior Year Abroad: Some Unexpected Results." Presentation made at the 1984 Northeast Conference, New York.

Index

NTC PROFESSIONAL MATERIALS

ACTFL Review

Published annually in conjunction with the American Council on the Teaching of Foreign Languages

Foreign Language Proficiency in the Classroom and Beyond, *ed. James*, Vol. 16 (1985)

Teaching for Proficiency, the Organizing Principle, *ed. Higgs*, Vol. 15 (1983)

Practical Applications of Research in Foreign Language Teaching, *ed. James*, Vol. 14 (1982)

Curriculum, Competence, and the Foreign Language Teacher, *ed. Higgs*, Vol. 13 (1981)

Action for the '80s: A Political, Professional, and Public Program for Foreign Language Education, *ed. Phillips*, Vol. 12 (1980)

The New Imperative: Expanding the Horizons of Foreign Language Education, *ed. Phillips*, Vol. 11 (1979)

Building on Experience—Building for Success, *ed. Phillips*, Vol. 10 (1978)

The Language Connection: From the Classroom to the World, *ed. Phillips*, Vol. 9 (1977)

An Integrative Approach to Foreign Language Teaching: Choosing Among the Options, *eds. Jarvis and Omaggio*, Vol. 8 (1976)

Perspective: A New Freedom, *ed. Jarvis*, Vol. 7 (1975)

The Challenge of Communication, *ed. Jarvis*, Vol. 6 (1974)

Foreign Language Education: A Reappraisal, *eds. Lange and James*, Vol. 4 (1972)

Foreign Language Education: An Overview, *ed. Birkmaier*, Vol. 1 (1969)

Professional Resources

Complete Guide to Exploratory Foreign Language Programs, *Kennedy and de Lorenzo*

Award-Winning Foreign Language Programs: Prescriptions for Success, *Sims and Hammond*

Living in Latin America: A Case Study in Cross-Cultural Communication, *Gorden*

Teaching Culture: Strategies for Intercultural Communication, *Seelye*

Individualized Foreign Language Instruction, *Grittner and LaLeike*

Oral Communication Testing, *Linder*

Transcription and Transliteration, *Wellisch*

ABC's of Languages and Linguistics

 For further information or a current catalog, write:
National Textbook Company
4255 West Touhy Avenue
Lincolnwood, Illinois 60646-1975 U.S.A.